Dreamed up Reality

Diving into mind to uncover
the astonishing hidden tale
of nature

Dreamed up Reality

Diving into mind to uncover
the astonishing hidden tale
of nature

Bernardo Kastrup

BOOKS

Winchester, UK
Washington, USA

First published by O-Books, 2011
iff Books is an imprint of John Hunt Publishing Ltd., No. 3 East Street, Alresford,
Hampshire SO24 9EE, UK
office1@jhpbooks.net
www.johnhuntpublishing.com

For distributor details and how to order please visit the 'Ordering' section on our website.

ISBN: 978 1 84694 525 0
978 1 84694 933 3 (ebook)

A CIP catalogue record for this book is available from the British Library.

Design: Stuart Davies

Figures 2, 5, and 9 to 18, copyright Bernardo Kastrup 2010
Figure 4 copyright Natalia Vorontsova 2010
Figures 1, 3, and 6 to 8, copyright by their respective copyright owners

UK: Printed and bound by CPI Group (UK) Ltd, Croydon, CR0 4YY
US: Printed and bound by Thomson Shore, 7300 West Joy Road, Dexter, MI 48130

We operate a distinctive and ethical publishing philosophy in all
areas of our business, from our global network of authors to
production and worldwide distribution.

CONTENTS

Other books by Bernardo Kastrup

Rationalist Spirituality: An exploration of the meaning of life and existence informed by logic and science

Meaning in Absurdity: What bizarre phenomena can tell us about the nature of reality

Why Materialism Is Baloney: How true skeptics know there is no death and fathom answers to life, the universe, and everything

Brief Peeks Beyond: Critical essays on metaphysics, neuroscience, free will, skepticism and culture

More Than Allegory: On religious myth, truth and belief

Coming March 2019
The Idea of the World: A multi-disciplinary argument for the mental nature of reality

To those gently trying to whisper us out of slumber

Imagine the amazement of Christopher Columbus upon discovering the New World, with its exotic fauna, flora, and seemingly alien natives...

Imagine the wonder of Marco Polo as he labored along the Silk Road, becoming immersed in cultures and costumes unknown...

Imagine the awe of Neil Armstrong and Edwin "Buzz" Aldrin upon watching the Earth from the surface of the moon...

...none of it can equal, in power or marvel, the sheer adventure of closing one's eyes and diving deep into one's own mind to *remember* that which is beyond language, time, and space.

Of all the usual labels with which our culture categorizes works of literature, like "science," "philosophy," or "fiction," maybe the one that best characterizes the work you now have in your hands is simply *art*. But "a kind of art whose medium is *ideas*; an art form that, although expressed in words like a work of fiction, engages in intense flirtation with the here and now; so intense in fact that, as in an obsessive love affair, it seeks to dissolve the boundaries between itself and the object of its affection. Such an art form thrives in the *possibility* that it is one with reality." (Chapter 11) Its products are born in the innermost recesses of one's own mind, where one witnesses the unspeakable and wonders: "Perhaps the apparently fixed mechanisms of nature are merely an epiphenomenon; an emergent property of the sympathetic harmonization of different imaginations, imagination itself being the true primary substance of reality. Perhaps the laws of physics can themselves be reduced to a fundamental metaphysics of psyche." (Chapter 7)

Chapter 1

The tale of an imaged universe

The magic of myth and imagination is an essential ingredient of our lives, at least during our formative years. When young, many of us were remarkably sensitive to the wondrous worlds of the imagination. To immerse our young selves in their enchantment, all we needed was a long, dark winter morning, a warm blanket, and a comfortable bed. Amazing journeys could then begin through alternative universes of light, flight, and unending possibilities, populated by creatures of many characters and intentions. How *real* that all seemed to be. We knew, because we were so told, that those worlds were not truly "real," but such learned notions did not seem to diminish the intensity of the experience. Authors, philosophers, and artists have since time immemorial played with this subjectively hazy border between reality and imagination. In the late 20th century, perhaps no one has done so more skillfully than Jostein Gaarder in his literary masterpiece, "Sophie's World."[1]

Just *what* is real? How do we *define* real? The world each one of us lives in is the subjective inner world of our own perceptions and other experiences. If our reality is the experiences we go through in our lives, then a private, imaginary experience is just as real as an objective one shared with other individuals. The most obvious difference between these two categories seems to be the following: in a private, imaginary experience the story is unconstrained; on the other hand, in an objective experience the story is somehow synchronized across the individuals sharing the experience so they all witness the same thing. The mechanisms for such synchronization are what we call the laws of nature, or the laws of physics. Such laws provide seemingly external constraints that ensure all participants share a common, consistent experience we call reality.

The mainstream scientific worldview adopted in our modern society informs us that the laws of physics are external to us and that we are merely a result of their operation. We are also informed that the laws of physics are objective; that is, that they operate regardless of our belief in, as well as of our under-standing and perception of, them. As such, they provide a robust and reliable, external synchronization mechanism that ensures certain modalities of our experiences are consistent across individuals. This way, when awake and in ordinary states of consciousness, most of us agree on what we experience together. In fact, it is this very consistency across the experiences of multiple individuals that motivates us to believe in an objective reality "out there," operating regardless of our beliefs and worldviews.

But there is circularity in this line of reasoning. To illustrate it, allow me to tell you a little tale about an imaginary universe called "Dhiiverse"...

Dhiiverse is a universe different from ours in one very funda-mental way: there, the laws of physics are not fixed and objective. Instead, reality is a projection of thought patterns imagined by its conscious inhabitants. These thought patterns, while being imagined, are projected onto a multi-dimensional fabric of space-time. Life in Dhiiverse is life in a kind of palpable, semi-autonomous, enduring dream. The inhabitants of Dhiiverse are people much like us: our brothers and sisters of a parallel reality, if you will. But, unlike us, the reality they live in is a complex amalgamation of their collective dreams.

Indeed, because different people in Dhiiverse concurrently project different and often conflicting thought patterns onto the same fabric of space-time, the resulting reality is a complex, emergent,[2] non-linear combination of the various scenarios being imagined. The combination itself manifests as a pattern, but one that may bear little resemblance to the original, individual thought patterns imagined by its co-creators. The mechanisms and causal influences behind the combination of thought patterns are transcendent, remaining amongst the greatest mysteries of Dhiiversian cosmology. Dhiiversian worlds are mystifying paintings of many painters.

Most inhabitants of Dhiiverse have an instinctive and visceral need for closure. They long for the definitive explanations of the phenomena they perceive and undergo. *They do not know that everything they experience is the compound result of their dreams*; the compound result of what their own minds are projecting onto the fabric of space-time around them. After all, what they think they are imagining or aspiring for is, more often than not, unlike the emergent reality they perceive in their immediate surroundings. The painting they see is not the one they thought they had painted. Therefore, they have concluded long ago that reality must be an objective, stand-alone phenomenon existing outside of their control. Accepting this worldview, they long for an ability to predict what might happen next in their reality. They yearn to gain some degree of reassurance about their predicament as puppets of a dispassionate cosmic process.

Such yearnings have long ago translated into a strong and instinctive eagerness, on the part of most Dhiiversians, to try and learn from what they perceive in their surroundings. *Because of their need for closure, they innately expect consistency in all they experience.* If a Dhiiversian, in a prior occasion and circumstances, has perceived the manifestation of a certain pattern on a segment of space-time, she will remember it. Next time she finds herself under similar circumstances, she will instinctively expect to see that same pattern again. For instance, if once she saw a shiny dot of red light manifest in the fabric of space-time above an iridescent streak of deep blue, she will expect to see a red dot appear again next time she encounters a blue streak. In a way, she will have *learned* to expect the recurring manifestation of certain patterns every time she re-encounters the context and circumstances under which she perceived those patterns earlier. This very expectation of consistency leads to her imagining those patterns, albeit without being self-reflectively aware of it, when cued by the right circumstances, thereby actively contributing to their consistent manifestation in the fabric of space-time. Next time, she will imagine the brilliant red dot and project its manifestation above the iridescent blue line. *The inhabitant's own imagination therefore reinforces her learned expectations.*

Each confirmation of their *learned* cognitive models provides the inhabitants of Dhiiverse with a growing, albeit illusory, sense of closure. *Through their imagination, they create the very consistency they yearn to find.* And the more they believe in it, the stronger their expectations become, the more efficiently they visualize and project onto reality what they expect, and the more confirmation they get for their expectations. It is a magical, self-reinforcing cycle. Such dynamics provides reassurance of their ability to understand and predict their environment. However, it also leads to a growing sense of vulnerability; of being at the mercy of external, detached cosmic forces entirely outside of their control; of having no purpose or *raison d'être* in life.

Communication and the sharing of experiences are essential parts of Dhiiversian culture. In the course of their social lives, Dhiiversians observe together, under shared circumstances, the manifestation of common, emerging realities. Each of these emerging realities is the resulting combination of their interacting imagination processes. They all learn together to associate such emerging realities to the shared circumstances of their occurrences. In other words, they all learn that such or such circumstance leads to this or that manifested reality. They jointly cognize mere correlations – local, regular saliencies of an unspeakably broader pattern – as causal links. *The more*

Dhiiversians witness phenomena together, the more they build a common, shared set of cognitive models and expectations. The effect of this process is the spread of a common, learned set of expectations and a homogenization of the imagination. Different individuals eventually begin imagining and projecting very similar scenarios onto the fabric of space-time, for they have *learned* to have similar expectations about what they should witness. More and more, the emergent realities that actually manifest confirm their now shared expectations. Everybody begins to agree not only about what is going on, but also about what *will* be going on. Consistency takes over not only across time and space, but now also across individual minds.

Soon, reality begins to behave just like everyone expects it to behave. So much so that learned Dhiiversians, its scientists and empiricists, begin formalizing the consistent correlations observed between circumstances and manifested phenomena. They create models of these correlations, eventually enshrining these models with the status of "immutable laws;" such is the accuracy and robustness of their predictions. They invent the concepts of cause and effect to model the empirically observable correlations present in the manifested *pattern* of dreamed up reality. Their scientific view of the painting of reality is that a streak of blue *caused* the dot of shiny red pigment above it, since red dots appear reliably above blue lines across the canvas (except perhaps for a few atypical exceptions they assume can be explained away). Intricate models are developed to capture the "causal" relationships between dots, streaks, pigments, etc., with extraordinary and, in a way, amusing effectiveness. But no link is ever established to the *thought patterns* of the painters who actually laid everything out on the canvas; as it turns out, those seem not to be needed to consistently capture the dynamics of most observations. Indeed, the manifested reality that emerges in Dhiiverse is internally consistent *by construction*, given the innate yearnings for regularity and predictability that

5

characterized the mindset of its creators while in the process of creation. The learned Dhiiversians say: "Look how consistently reality behaves itself! Red dots practically always follow on top of blue streaks. This is proof that reality operates according to fixed and objective rules: blue streaks *must cause* red dots. Otherwise, we would expect there to be more randomness and unpredictability in their occurrences."

Armed with their remarkable models, the learned Dhiiversians become masters of the manipulation of their manifested world; for they empirically cracked the local, salient regularities encoded in the patterns of their now highly synchronized dreams. They become the ultimate expert commentators of their own painting, though they are completely blind to the fact that they are painting it themselves. They apply this expertise to the development of technology, which is then immediately put to use for the achievement of their many aspirations. First and foremost in the list of such aspirations: faster, broader, more frequent and efficient communication. As Dhiiversians communicate and share experiences faster and more widely than ever before, the emergent patterns of their reality crystallize like diamonds. *Dhiiversians all learn to dream the same dream.* By now, no Dhiiversian could ever fail to notice the patently obvious: Dhiiversian reality is an objective, deterministic, predicable in principle, rock-solid, stand-alone phenomenon.

All the while, the true physics of Dhiiverse has remained what it has always been: a physics of the imagination; a malleable and fluidic physics of dreams, more akin to water than to diamond. The fact that everyone decided to agree and expect the same things has never changed the inherently flexible character of what is *actually* going on. Only the *metaphysics of* Dhiiverse, governing the mysterious mechanisms by means of which the pattern of a shared reality emerges from inconsistent dreams, seems fixed an immutable. Yet, from the point of view of the average Dhiiversian, such ideas could not appear to be more abstract, irrelevant, or outright ridiculous. Dhiiversians feel like puppets in a cosmic play whose script they did not write or had a chance to influence. Such is the degree of accuracy with which they have succeeded in calibrating empirical models of manifested phenomena, they believe there cannot be any doubt that their world is indeed governed by those models. *All objective evidence available points at this inescapable conclusion; statistically, it cannot be a coincidence.* Only fools or deluded individuals would think otherwise.

Yet, some dare to resist the overwhelming consensus. Dhiiversian scientists scorn these few outcasts who make bizarre and demonstrably nonsensical claims; claims that all Dhiiversians live in a dreamed up world resulting directly from their synchronized imaginations; claims that the metaphysics of this synchronization is the only true, immutable, underlying rule governing existence, everything else being determined by thought in the acquiescent medium of their individual minds. Dhiiversian scientists challenge these outcasts to demonstrate, under controlled conditions, that they can break the established laws of physics of Dhiiverse. Naturally, the momentum behind the synchronized expectations pushing for the mainstream version of reality is now so formidable that no outcast, however determined to project a different reality he or she might be, can succeed in such a demonstration. Even though the outcasts are correct about the true nature of the *underlying* reality of Dhiiverse, *manifested* reality, which is the only one available to ordinary observation, will continue to be what the vast majority believes and projects it to be. The outcasts cannot, *precisely because they are correct*, demonstrate the validity of their thesis objectively. For this, they are not taken seriously by Dhiiversian scientists.

Yet, the outcasts do not scorn science. On the contrary: they admire scientific pursuit for its steady uncovering of the beauty and complexity of manifested nature. This, they believe,

7

provides indirect clues to the mysterious metaphysics of Dhiiverse and is essential for the proper contemplation of the painting of existence – the outcasts' most fulfilling pleasure. They also value the utilitarian role Dhiiversian science plays in enabling the development of Dhiiversian technology. However, unlike most Dhiiversians, they do not make the mistake of *extrapolating* the operational effectiveness of Dhiiversian science – its ability to model and anticipate the behavior of manifested things and processes – to ontology. In other words, to the outcasts, the models of Dhiiversian science are just that: mock-ups that work (red dots *do* mostly occur above blue streaks), not fundamental knowledge of the true nature of Dhiiversian reality. The outcasts know that what science calls causality is simply the visible manifestation of local regularities in an unfathomable, compound thought pattern. *There are many other, non-local, yet unrecognized regularities in that pattern.* They know that blue lines do not *cause* red dots – that supposedly being the final explanation of the phenomenon of red dots – but simply that this local correlation between lines and dots is an operationally useful one to model. To the outcasts of Dhiiverse, the models of science are to reality as a map is to the streets of a city: while the isomorphism of the map – that is, the correspondence of form between map and streets – is accurate and operationally useful for navigating around the city, the map informs us very little about how the city really came to being; about how and why its streets were laid out the way they were; and about what their true nature and purpose are.

But how could the outcasts intuit the underlying reality of Dhiiverse in the first place? After all, *nearly all* objective evidence, as perceived with their five senses, was entirely consistent with the mainstream view of an objective and deterministic physics.

Their secret was the following: they did not look for knowledge *outside* of themselves; that would have just

8

reaffirmed the illusory consensus already reigning in their civilization. Instead, they looked *inside* themselves. Initially through involuntary but mesmerizing dreams, and thereafter through purposeful meditation, the outcasts began diving deep into their own consciousnesses. Since the true reality of Dhiiverse had all along been a reality of *mind*, diving into *mind* gave them privileged access to aspects of that reality that remained elusive to others. To understand the art more intimately, they looked not at the painting, but into the mind of the painter.

In doing so, they gained direct awareness of larger portions of the fabric of space-time that was the natural canvas of their mental processes. *They realized that it had hidden dimensions not available to regular objective perception*, but only to non-ordinary states of consciousness. Because of that, entire segments of this hyper-dimensional, mental fabric of space-time were like blank canvases, largely free from the noise of the imaginations of others. The mainstream synchronization constraints of manifested reality had no hold in those spaces. When visiting such segments of space-time through introspective awareness, the outcasts of Dhiiverse realized that they could fashion the entire reality of those spaces at will. Yet, the reality so fashioned was nearly as concrete, palpable, and enduring as the so-called objective – that is, synchronized – reality.

Those unclaimed segments of hyper-dimensional space-time real estate became their laboratories of subjective experimentation. As true empiricists, by applying reason and logic to interpreting their experimental results, the outcasts of Dhiiverse began constructing not physical, but *meta*physical models not of the manifested, but of the *underlying* reality of their universe. In their metaphysics, they took feeble early steps in the direction of comprehending *the thought pattern of thought patterns*; the One, the Source, the Transcendence that orchestrated the combination of all free-willed dreams in the manifestation of a chosen, shared reality. They understood that *this shared reality was a common playing field of shared experience, collaboratively built by all its players, and that it served a profound purpose.* They understood that their greatest and most valuable new insight was that they, and their fellow Dhiiversians, did not know nearly as much as they had thought they did about how the universe is put together. There was not to be closure, but simply appreciative contemplation. And that became their most sensitive secret...

From very early on, the outcasts of Dhiiverse knew that, as a very consequence of their own metaphysics, they had little chance of ever providing *objective* proof of their thesis. The only way others could be made to understand what was meant was through *their own direct experience* of it. The others had to voluntarily immerse themselves into the ocean of their own consciousnesses in order to glimpse at the *underlying pattern* that revealed the truth.

It was the hope of the outcasts of Dhiiverse that, through a discrete, non-confrontational, open, honest, but also judicious and serious effort to divulge some of their ideas, they could excite the curiosity of others; perhaps of those whose intuition had already been suggesting that something was not quite right about the mainstream model of reality. The goal of the outcasts had never been to *prove* their case objectively, but simply to show an alternative possibility to those willing to hear their case with a critical but open mind.

The conclusion of the Dhiiversian story – a story driven and enriched by the fertility of the imagination of its participants – is yet to be told.

Chapter 2

The insufficiency of science for uncovering the true nature of reality

One of my strongest early memories is that of suddenly realizing, as a young boy, that I was an entity separate from the world around me. For a period of perhaps several months, I would often catch myself thinking in sheer amazement: "I am me... I am not the other people or things I see... how peculiar!" Indeed, such a realization was most curious and strange. I was a separate entity and, most disturbing of all, I had apparently never been anything or anybody else. How bizarre and counter-intuitive, yet logically inescapable, such conclusion was. I can still vaguely recall the disquieting sense of disappointment and claustrophobia that accompanied it. Such was the birth of what I now understand to be my ego: that which defines me as the personal subject of my experiences.

As the years passed, it was that very ego that became a fundamental tool for the pursuit of what, for me, has been the most intriguing, interesting, important, and urgent question of all: *What is the true nature of reality?* Just what *is* reality and what is the nature of our condition as conscious entities within it? It was the ego that allowed me to pursue an investigation *of* reality in an objective manner: as an investigator who could impartially observe nature, thereby making inferences about its operating mechanisms. Science seemed to offer the correct procedures and tools for that investigation, so I pursued science for several years, secretly hoping to answer that ultimate question before my time here would expire. Having understood how science actually works, I realized its limitations as a method for the pursuit of ontology; that is, the study of the true nature of being and existence. Indeed, science models the *relationships between things*, but is surprisingly limited in clarifying their underlying nature. It leaves out the truly important questions, as articulated so eloquently by Terence McKenna when he commented that "we human beings must admit that ours is a peculiar situation: having been born, we are autonomous, open chemical systems that maintain themselves through metabolism at a point far from equilibrium. And we are creatures of thought. What is that? What are the three dimensions? What is energy? We find ourselves in the strange position of being alive. [...] So what is it for? Spenser and Shakespeare, quantum theory and the cave paintings at Altamira. Who are we? What is history? And what does it push toward?"[1] Science cannot answer this kind of questions without immediately raising other, similar questions. Since it captures only relationships, its answers ultimately entail circularity and are not fundamentally satisfying.

Indeed, science is the quintessential *third-person* investigatory method. The key historical premises of the scientific method are two-fold: first, one must assume that there is an objective reality "out there" that does not depend on one as observer of it. In other words, one must assume that the world would still go on strictly according to the laws of physics even if there were nobody looking at it. Second, one must assume that one's first-person observations of reality are unreliable and suspicious. After all, our senses are imperfect: what I see or hear may not really correspond to what is "out there." Therefore, in science, sufficient third-person confirmation of one's observations is paramount. In practice, this translates into the need for the repetition of experiments by multiple individuals or groups, with consistent resulting observations, before a scientific model can be declared truthful. *In science, the definition of truth is that which is independently but consistently reported by a sufficient number of observers under controlled observation conditions.* Since we know that all observations are subjective in nature, and that we have no direct access to an objective truth "out there," *a central assumption in science is that objective truth corresponds to the statistical consistency of individual subjective observations.* When the particularities and idiosyncrasies of individual observations are significant enough, they invalidate an overall conclusion. Otherwise, they are discarded as statistical noise around the averaged-out observation that is then taken as the reflection of objective truth. Either way, the scientific method does not attribute ontological value to the idiosyncrasies of individual subjective experience.

Notice that the second premise is a consequence of the first: the assumed unreliability of first-person observation is itself grounded in the assumption that reality is objective. It is the assumed objectivity of reality that provides a neutral reference against which one's first-person observations can be judged. If I look at a traffic sign and observe it to be green, that observation can be judged against the objective reality of the state of the traffic sign: if it is indeed green, my observation is correct; otherwise, I am probably color-blind and a liability on the roads, facts that the traffic sign cares nothing about. If not for the assumed objectivity of reality – that is, its independence from conscious observation – reality itself would be a subjective concept dependent on whoever experiences it. Since the world does not *seem* to work that way, the premise of objectivity is ubiquitous.

Here, a brief detour from our main line of argumentation is necessary. Quantum mechanics is often cited as a segment of science wherein the assumption of objectivity has collapsed. According to quantum theory, the observer inherently interferes with what is observed, thereby somehow creating his or her own reality. We hear that objective reality, independent of the observer, does not exist in a quantum world, something often called the "observer effect." While the current state of scientific understanding indeed seems to confirm the observer effect, and while it is a central theme of this book that it may be, in a certain way, correct, it is also true that the mainstream position of science remains consistent with its original premises: even in the case of quantum mechanics, the models of mainstream science, with the advancement of our understanding of quantum decoherence and interpretations of quantum reality based on parallel universes,[2] have managed to preserve at least the possibility that objectivity is a property of nature.

It is important that, in any discourse about the underlying truths of nature, one carefully avoid the temptation to illegitimately hijack the mainstream positions of science. Such temptation stems from the fact that, according to the standards of our materialist society, whose origins go back to the European Enlightenment, a statement or position is only respectable and deserving of belief if its derivation has been grounded on the scientific method. Because of this historical fact, those who attempt to promote something – be it a product, a technique, or a theory – often seek to associate that something to science, precariously as it may be.

The European Enlightenment embodied a reaction to the superstition and arbitrary morals that had ruled European society for centuries. After all, superstition and arbitrary morals were creations of men, not the inherent properties of nature sought as final truths. Science attempted to dispel nonsensical assertions about reality by the simple use of *reason* and *observation*. Overtime, that led to the formalization of what has become a very clearly defined and strict process: the scientific method. The reliance of societies worldwide today on the scientific method is explainable by science's spectacular success in modeling nature for engineering purposes; that is, by science's efficacy in leveraging the materials and forces of nature in the service of humans. It is, after all, undeniable how the application of the scientific method has improved the length and quality of our lives over the centuries.

The effectiveness of the scientific method rests on its clear and strict application. Saying that something is scientific must, therefore, entail strict compliance to that method. Nonetheless, often things popularly purported today to be scientific are not scientific at all. As physicist Richard Feynman once asserted, following merely the *forms* of science does not entail compliance to the scientific method any more than the "cargo cults" of pacific islanders entailed the air delivery of cargo.[3] True science requires much more than white coats or the use of scientific jargon. *True science requires staunch and systematic skepticism about one's own hypothesis until the only reasonable alternative left – in the framework of the reigning paradigm of the time – is that such a hypothesis be true.*

So does that mean that assertions about nature that are not strictly grounded on the scientific method are valueless? To answer "yes" to this question would logically require at least two elements: first, that the scientific method be *effective*; and second, that the scientific method be *sufficient* to explore *all* aspects of nature. There is no doubt about the correctness of the first statement. But there are at least two ways in which the second statement is false.

As discussed above, the scientific method is grounded in the premises of the objectivity of reality (a philosophical position often called "realism") and the unreliability of first-person observation, the latter following from the former. According to the scientific method, an observation is only acceptable as true if objectified – that is, quantified – and corroborated by a sufficient number of other independent observations. Largely due to its roots as a reaction to superstition, the scientific method is fundamentally skeptical of one's own subjective perceptions, placing all ontological value on an assumed objective reality. Yet, the existence of an objective, external reality cannot be proven beyond doubt, for we are all confined to our own individual perceptions and private inner worlds. Even the observations of nature reported by other people are themselves but elements of our own captive inner worlds.[4] As Robert Lanza put it, "living in an age dominated by science, we have come more and more to believe in an objective, empirical reality and in the goal of reaching a complete understanding of that reality. [...] But we're fooling ourselves. Most of these comprehensive theories are no more than stories that fail to take into account one crucial factor: we are creating them. It is the biological creature that makes observations, names what it observes, and creates stories. Science has not succeeded in confronting the element of existence that is at once most familiar and most mysterious – conscious experience."[5] Therefore, science seems to leave out a legitimate avenue for exploring nature: that of a purely first-person method wherein one dives into the depths and inner recesses of one's own consciousness. Indeed, many aspects of our private inner worlds are ineffable and cannot be objectified. It is conceivable that such inner worlds, through subjective perception mechanisms not yet scientifically understood, may give us access to aspects of nature no less ontologically valid than anything objectively verifiable, but which are inherently beyond the scope of a third-person, quantified approach. Since our inner worlds are, beyond any doubt, a part of nature, this is the first way in which science is an insufficient method for exploring nature.

The second way in which science is insufficient is its inability to capture the underlying essence of things and processes in and of themselves. Again, the scientific method allows one to make models of the relationships observed in nature, but is fundamentally limited when it comes to establishing what the elements of nature are per se. A model is an abstract mechanism whose elements and dynamics merely *correspond* to elements and dynamics of nature in an isomorphic manner. But models provide us no access to nature itself. The making of an accurate model allows us to predict and explain natural phenomena in an abstract, quantified framework, but not to make assertions about their intrinsic reality. Indeed, a scientific model is as far removed from reality as a computer-based flight simulator is removed from real flight: one would hardly claim that a flight simulation, no matter how accurate, *is* flight. Think of String Theory, for example: it models nature according to imaginary, abstract, mathematically described "strings" that oscillate in certain ways, such modes of oscillation corresponding to observed phenomena of nature in an isomorphic manner. But it leaves out the obvious ontological question: *Just what are those strings?*

British philosopher Dr. Ray Tallis once eloquently captured the limitations of the scientific method. As he put it, "science begins when we escape our subjective, first-person experiences into objective measurement. [...] Thus measurement takes us further from experience and the phenomena of subjective consciousness to a realm where things are described in abstract but quantitative terms. To do its work, physical science has to discard 'secondary qualities', such as colour, warmth or cold, taste – in short, the basic contents of consciousness. [...] Physical science is about the marginalisation, or even the disappearance, of phenomenal appearance."[6] Yet the *only* world we live in is a world of color, warmth, cold, taste, etc. By abstracting away from this first-person perspective, science restricts itself to a utilitarian role as enabler of technology and engineering. It ends up having nothing to say about the true nature of what we actually perceive in consciousness, which is the sole carrier of reality as far as we *can* know. Therefore, while science has an incalculably valuable role to play in our society as the enabler of technology, to truly understand the nature of our condition we need more than science.

What, then, might a method of investigation *complementary* to science look like? The very premises of the scientific method give us very clear clues. Indeed, if science is grounded in the premise that reality is objective, what avenues of investigation could be explored if one assumes, instead, that reality is fundamentally subjective? If science neglects the unique and idiosyncratic nature of first-person experience as irrelevant statistical noise, what might those very idiosyncrasies then reveal when assumed to be valid and studied in depth? Strictly speaking, these assumptions are even more parsimonious than the premises of science, for they do not postulate the existence of anything beyond the contents of consciousness. Such considerations all point to a common direction: that of an investigation of nature through the exploration of one's own mental landscape. I will call this method "subjective exploration," contrasting it to the "objective exploration" entailed by science, just to have a compact label to refer to later.

The question now is: just *why* should one believe that subjective exploration can provide *new* knowledge about the true nature of reality? After all, an exploration of our own mental landscape seems fundamentally restricted to whatever information or associations are *already* encoded in our brains. Learning *new* things about reality, on the other hand, must entail downloading knowledge into our brains that was *not* there before. How could we download new knowledge into our brains by looking inside our own minds?

The hypothesis here, which we will elaborate on extensively in the next chapter, is the following: through mechanisms yet unknown to science, our minds have *direct* access to a largely untapped repository of knowledge about reality. Under the right circumstances, we can gain direct awareness of aspects of nature inaccessible through objective means, thereby tapping into knowledge not previously present in the structures of the brain. What originally led me to give some credit to this apparently implausible possibility was an earlier realization that some people seemed able, through a form of direct insight, to arrive at the same realizations that had cost me years to formulate through objective, rational analysis. Once I had accepted this possibility, I carried out my own experiments of subjective exploration. Such experiments, described at length in upcoming chapters, convinced me of the possibility that a deep exploration of mind could indeed grant access to knowledge about the true nature of nature that was either new or had been forgotten.

Still, in order to ground and make sense of this hypothesis, we need to postulate a reasonable and believable mechanism, speculative as it may be, by means of which mind could gain direct access to aspects of reality otherwise inaccessible to objective investigation. A tentative model for just one such mechanism is described in the next chapter.

Before we move on, though, an important observation must be made. Science, as a method for the exploration of nature, makes use of many tools. Amongst these tools are *reason, logic,* and *empiricism*. But these tools are not the exclusive domain of the scientific method. In fact, they predate science by millennia. Therefore, one can legitimately use the tools of reason, logic, and experimentation while departing from strict compliance to the specific formulations and premises entailed by the scientific method. In doing so, *one is no longer doing science,* but may still very well be correctly and fruitfully applying reason, logic, and empiricism to their full extent. It is my hope that this book, while not at all attempting to be scientific, is indeed well grounded in reason, logic, clarity of thought, and on experiments relevant to its hypotheses.

Chapter 3

A field of mind as a universal repository of knowledge

In 2001, a remarkable medical case came to the attention of the scientific community.[1] A 51-year-old male from England was admitted to hospital with a sudden, severe headache. Scans revealed multiple cerebral artery aneurysms, which were causing hemorrhage in the brain. The patient – named Tommy – was subjected to surgery and subsequently released from hospital.

Tommy was a builder who reported having, prior to this event, a short temper, an aggressive personality, and no interest in creative arts. Yet, about two weeks after his surgery, Tommy began what was to become years of prolific artistic production. His works included poetry, drawing, painting, and sculpture, all of surprising quality. His obsession with art led him to cover the walls, floors, and ceilings of his house several times over with paintings. As he claimed, *each element of his drawings wanted to explode into something more*, in a never-ending stream of artistic inspiration and creative insight. It was as if Tommy's brain were being constantly flooded with impressions and images from a source yet to be identified. Somehow, the physical effects of the hemorrhage and subsequent surgery on the structure and function of his brain opened a valve to a major pipeline of impressions and inspiration.

Dr. Mark Lythgoe, the scientist who investigated this case most closely, used a metaphor to explain what happened.[2] According to him, two major processes are at work in our brains all the time: one is an excitatory process, responsible for the influx of new ideas; the other is an inhibitory process, called "latent inhibition," responsible for focusing our attention on the perceptions that are most practical and important to our immediate priorities and survival. He speculated that, in Tommy's case, the inhibitory process had been damaged. With his latent inhibition diminished, Tommy then struggled to handle all the uninhibited impressions that kept flooding into awareness. What he then did was to create art. Scientists postulate that the excitatory process is, somehow, a brain-based process explainable by, and reducible to, the physiological mechanisms of the brain. However, as compulsory as it may seem to be according to the materialistic paradigm, this is still an *assumption*, for the implied mechanisms have not been pinned down.

Tommy's case could, instead, be interpreted according to the "mind at large" metaphysical model popularized by acclaimed author Aldous Huxley and eminent philosopher Charlie Dunbar Broad in the 1950s: that mind is intrinsically capable of remembering all that has ever happened and perceiving all that happens in the entire universe. The nervous system would have then evolved to sort through this abundance of impressions and filter out everything that was not useful to the immediate survival of the physical body.[3] What becomes available to awareness after this filtering process is mostly the inputs from our five senses, which correlate well with the location in space and time of the physical body and, therefore, are most practical to its survival. Perhaps our five senses have themselves evolved not to *produce* information, but as parts of a *selection and emphasis mechanism* responsible for picking out impressions, anyway available to consciousness, based on a criterion of *locality* in both space and time that was most relevant to body survival. Such metaphysics echoes the philosophies of several schools of mysticism and spirituality, particularly those from the East, which claim that consciousness is a unified field capable – by its very non-local, field-like nature – of extra-sensory perception across time and space.

My own metaphysics, as discussed in my earlier work "Rationalist Spirituality,"[4] points in the same direction. I have argued – though I cannot repeat the complete substantiation of that complex argument here – that we are all, in principle, capable of accessing a universal record of all conscious impressions ever registered by any conscious entity. I have called such record a "universal memory of qualia."

What all these metaphysical speculations suggest is that the process of latent inhibition is the only one firmly grounded on the physical nervous system. The excitatory process responsible for creativity, on the other hand, may not be entirely brain-based. Instead, it may entail the non-local influx of impressions and knowledge inherent to consciousness. According to this interpretation, in Tommy's case a physical perturbation of normal brain structures and operation may have compromised his latent inhibition, causing his brain to lose its ability to filter the influx of impressions from the universal memory of qualia. One wonders if a partial and temporary disablement of these filters could also be achieved on a safe, controlled, voluntary basis, without brain damage.

If these speculations are correct, then *the most direct and efficient way to acquire knowledge about reality is through a partial and temporary disablement of the filtering mechanisms of the brain.* Indeed, as we will see in the next chapter, there is an abundance of empirical evidence that, through technologies like meditation, yoga, hypnosis, prayer, lucid dreaming, shamanic rituals, sensory and sleep deprivation, fasting or other ordeals, etc., people throughout history have been able to perturb their evolved brain filters and temporarily tap into a universal source of *direct* knowledge.

We can further speculate that the direct impressions received in such non-ordinary states of consciousness can be partially imprinted onto the physical brain through collapse of the brain's quantum wave function. This would allow for the imprinting of extra-sensory impressions onto the brain without violating causality or any of the known laws of physics, like energy and momentum conservation. Scientists like Henry Stapp[5] and Roger Penrose[6] have proposed various concrete mechanisms by means of which such imprinting could take place.

It is my view that the repository of experiences and direct knowledge entailed by the universal memory of qualia is not necessarily physical in nature. When stating this, I do not mean to imply substance dualism, but simply that the mechanisms behind such record may be grounded in aspects of nature not amenable to scientific investigation and not even touched upon by our materialist models. That said, there have been attempts to find a physical basis for a form of universal, non-local information storage. To mention only one prominent example, eminent Hungarian philosopher Ervin László sought to link an "Akashic field" of universal information to the vacuum state of quantum field theory.[7]

So the hypothesis I am postulating here is the following: consciousness is a non-local field phenomenon not caused by, nor reducible to, the brain, but simply associated in some manner with the brain. All understanding and knowledge ever registered by a conscious entity survives *ad infinitum* in the field of consciousness as permanent experiences, or qualia. Therefore, all universal knowledge is, in principle, accessible by any conscious entity. It is the local attention filters of the nervous system, evolved as a consequence of earlier survival advantages, which prevent us from accessing this universal repository of knowledge. But through perturbations of ordinary brain operation, which partially and temporarily disable or bypass some of these filters, one can gain awareness of it. The consequent input of knowledge can be imprinted onto the brain – where it is later interpreted, articulated, and reported – through a process of quantum wave function collapse.

While currently not corroborated by science, this hypothesis is logical and consistent with empirical evidence. Importantly, it also does *not* contradict current scientific fact – perhaps only scientific prejudices – for science today does not have even tentative explanations for the phenomenon of consciousness. Indeed, in what is often referred to as the "explanatory gap" or the "hard problem of consciousness," we have not been able to articulate even a tentative model for reducing consciousness to supposedly non-conscious material substrates.[8] As philosopher David Chalmers put it, referring to earlier work by renowned physicist Steven Weinberg, "despite the power of physical theory, the existence of consciousness does not seem to be derivable from physical laws."[9]

The "mind at large" hypothesis formulated in this chapter will be our starting point and conceptual framework for the investigation that follows. I do not ask you to simply believe in this hypothesis at this point, but just that you maintain an open mind about it. In the next chapter, we will look at some of the technologies for awareness expansion that have been used in different human societies throughout history. By "awareness expansion" I mean any method through which one can partially and temporarily bypass the brain's attention filters and gain direct awareness of the universal repository of knowledge postulated above.

Chapter 4

The technologies of mind exploration

As Galileo Galilei needed a telescope to explore the heavens and Antoni van Leeuwenhoek a microscope to explore the world of microorganisms, one needs an "innerscope" to explore the inner landscapes of one's own consciousness. Throughout history, different civilizations, societies, and cultures have used different innerscope technologies for bypassing the brain's attention filters, thereby gaining awareness of non-local knowledge about the underlying nature of reality. In the next paragraphs, I list some of these technologies. I am not an expert in any of them, so the descriptions below are limited and intended merely as a quick reference. *This is not a guide for reaching non-ordinary states of consciousness, or a guide of any other sort for that matter, and it does not contain advice, instructions, recipes, formulae or procedures of any kind.* Readers interested in any particular technique should do further research before attempting to use it, for there are inherent risks associated with the use of each one of them. The proper evaluation of the suitability of each one of these techniques for one's purposes and circumstances, and the eventual application of these techniques, both require thorough background research that cannot be limited to the information provided below. Finally, the list below is also admittedly incomplete, which reflects my limited knowledge of the subject rather than personal favoritism or prejudice against any particular approach.

Meditation, in its countless forms, is the quintessential and time-proven technology of awareness expansion. It has been practiced for millennia both in and out of a religious context. The goal of the practice is to steer our thought processes from the reactive, reflexive mode in which we live most of our waking lives, to a more relaxed state of inner awareness and receptiveness. Meditation generally involves techniques for disciplining one's thoughts and attention mechanisms. For example, the technique used by one of the best-known schools of meditation in the West, the so-called school of "Transcendental Meditation,"[1] comprises the mental repetition of a sound called a "mantra," which aims, among other things, at focusing one's attention. Particle physicist Dr. John Hagelin, a life-long meditator and alumnus, like me, of the European Organization for Nuclear Research (CERN), has proposed that deep meditative states bring one's awareness in direct contact with a unified, non-local, underlying field of consciousness at the basis of all reality. He went on to identify this field of consciousness with the "unified field" entailed by the grand-unification theories of physics,[2] one of which is of his own co-authorship.[3]

A thorough review of 75 scientific studies on meditation has identified non-ordinary states of awareness as one of its main psychological effects.[4] It is this very effect that has been sought after and leveraged by mystics of all ages for the achievement of enlightenment and for accessing universal knowledge. However, it should also be noted that the same study has identified potential psychological side-effects of meditation, including relaxation-induced anxiety, disorientation, and mild dissociation. Therefore, despite our natural inclination to consider inconsequential a technique that entails purely the self-manipulation of one's attention mechanisms, *meditation clearly seems to work* and, thus, should be approached with earnestness.

Meditation can be practiced by itself or used in combination with other technologies of awareness expansion, as listed below. In general, most – if not all – effective attempts at non-ordinary states of consciousness are likely to entail meditation in one form or another. After all, regardless of the other technologies potentially being deployed, some degree of intentional control over one's own attention is essential in any thoughtful exploration of nature, objective or subjective.

Another technology of awareness expansion closely related to meditation is *visualization*. It entails more deliberate control of one's own mental imagery and feelings. While meditation tends to be more passive and receptive, visualization entails the very active and purposeful control of one's stream of thoughts. Visualization has been a foundation technique for the achievement of mystical insight in traditional schools of Esotericism, like the Rosicrucian school. In a now rare book titled "Messages from the Celestial Sanctum,"[5] French Rosicrucian Raymond Bernard walks the reader through his visualization technique. He also illustrates the results achieved by articulating and reporting the "messages" – that is, the insights – he received through the application of this technique. The key to the technique is the use of one's focused imagination to create and project onto the screen of one's own mind a dreamed up scenario conducive to receiving the kind of guidance or knowledge being sought. Like a designed dream, at the pinnacle of the visualization process one is meant to become so immersed in the scenario chosen that the process becomes autonomous, no longer requiring active effort. It appears that it is at this point that a knowledge influx is received.

The most natural criticism against visualization as a technique for exploration and discovery is that it may embody an obvious form of self-deception. After all, one may be creating, through active application of the imagination, the very "knowledge" that one believes to be receiving. However, the premise is that the imagery being visualized simply *dresses, clothes* the knowledge being received in forms and symbols that can be recognized and interpreted by the rational mind, the underlying knowledge itself coming from outside the brain. As Bernard explains, at the culmination of the visualization one must let go of all intentional effort, becoming passive and receptive to the influx of impressions. This influx can last anywhere between a fraction of a second and several minutes, or even longer. In all cases, however, it seems that it is only *after* the completion of the intuitive influx that one is able to begin articulating the knowledge received according to regular brain processes and language structures.

The technologies of awareness expansion discussed thus far entail no more than the purposeful manipulation of one's own mental processes. Therefore, in principle, they can be practiced anywhere, fairly inconspicuously. That said, doing it in an environment of sensory deprivation seems to be by far the easiest way to achieve an unambiguous influx of impressions. Distractions in the form of light or noise can make it very difficult to tune in to those signals. In my own experience, meditation and visualization, when used for the purposes discussed here, are best practiced in isolation, in a quiet and dark room. An even more effective alternative, when one has the means to do so safely, may be to practice these techniques out in nature, in an isolated place, at night.

Another technology for achieving non-ordinary states of consciousness that naturally requires silence and darkness is *lucid dreaming*. Dreams are, in themselves, non-ordinary states of consciousness. Psychiatrist Carl Jung, founder of analytical psychology, saw dreams as a way to access the collective unconscious.[6] The latter, he described in the following way: "In addition to our immediate consciousness, which is of a thoroughly personal nature [...], there exists a second psychic system of a collective, universal, and impersonal nature which is identical in all individuals."[7] Clearly, the collective unconscious is somewhat related to the idea of a universal memory of qualia. To the extent that dreams can tap into the collective unconscious, they could entail a state of consciousness suitable for accessing knowledge unavailable to objective perception. Moreover, a careful scientific study, carried out in 2004 by Harvard

University's Dr. Daniel Wegner and collaborators, shows that dreams seem particularly effective at bringing to awareness mental content that has been suppressed in ordinary states of consciousness. In the conclusion of their paper, Dr. Wegner wrote that "suppressed thoughts apparently assert themselves in dreams whether they are about wished-for targets or not. The rebound of suppressed thoughts in dreams may be interpretable in terms of the influence of changes in brain activation during REM sleep on mental control processes. The relative deactivation of prefrontal areas associated with executive control that occurs during dreaming could undermine the effectiveness of the suppression operating process."[8] So the dream state in general seems promising as a vehicle for subjective exploration, given the "mind at large" hypothesis formulated in the previous chapter. What makes a *lucid dream* even more interesting is that, in it, the dreamer: *is perfectly aware that he or she is in a dream; preserves his or her ability to reason logically and critically about what is being experienced; and can even exert control over the unfolding of the dream through visualization.* It is these features that allow one to make *purposeful* and *critical* use of the dream state as a tool of subjective exploration. Lucid dreams seem also to be less difficult to remember afterwards, an important advantage over regular dreams when one plans on extracting lasting conclusions from the experience.

Though lucid dreams can happen spontaneously, they can also be purposefully and systematically induced. As such, they can be initiated either from a normal dream ("Dream-Initiated Lucid Dream," or DILD) or directly from a regular waking state ("Wake-Initiated Lucid Dream," or WILD). Drifting into a lucid dream directly from a waking state, without any loss of awareness in between, can be both very disconcerting and highly gratifying; one may suddenly find oneself already fully immersed in an alternative reality, while in full possession of one's reasoning and analytical skills. This, in my view, is a truly unparalleled, confounding, and ecstatic experience. It provides an unambiguous demonstration of the power of the psyche to create a coherent, seemingly autonomous reality for its own experience. People who have never had a clear lucid dream may be skeptical about it. It may then be interesting to note that lucid dreams have been scientifically demonstrated to be a fact.[9]

Psychophysiologist Dr. Stephen LaBerge has been an influential researcher and educator in the field of lucid dreaming. He is the founder of "The Lucidity Institute," an organization dedicated to the research of lucid dreams, the development of techniques for inducing them, and the education of people interested in attempting lucid dreaming. Dr. LaBerge has written many articles and books on lucid dreams, exploring their main characteristics, potential risks, and techniques for achieving lucid dream states. A thorough guide for anyone interested in the subject is his book "Exploring the World of Lucid Dreaming."[10]

Unlike meditation, visualization, and lucid dreaming, *Yoga* is not a purely mental practice. It is a time-honored technology of awareness expansion that entails breathing techniques and the performance of specific physical movements and postures. In Western society, it has been often used as a mere physical exercise for its widely recognized health benefits, including psychological ones.[11] However, for the spiritual seeker, yoga is a physical aid to the practice of meditation. It helps the meditator reach non-ordinary states of awareness by, for instance, conditioning the organism in such a way that mental or physical distractions do not become an impediment to introspection. As with any physical activity, caution and medical orientation are advisable when practicing yoga, in case of pre-existing medical conditions.

Brain entrainment, on the other hand, is a technique to induce the synchronization of brain waves with an external, rhythmic stimulus of a chosen frequency.[12] The stimulus usually takes the form of an audio-visual signal generated by a so-called "mind machine." A mind machine, sometimes also called a "psycho walkman," typically comprises a control unit, headphones, and a pair of goggles housing light-emitting diodes. Some mind machines are enhanced with sophisticated biofeedback mechanisms that, based on the user's biophysical responses, adjust on-the-fly the frequency of the stimulus being generated. When wearing a mind machine, one's perceptions become dominated by the rhythmic pulses played through the headphones and the flashing lights displayed in the goggles. The idea is the following: different states of consciousness, including deeply meditative states, are associated with brain waves of specific frequency ranges; by focusing on the rhythmic sounds and flashing lights of a mind machine, one's brain waves fall naturally in step with the external stimulus; therefore, when this external stimulus is chosen so as to correspond to the frequency of deeply meditative states, it helps induce such states on the user. Indeed, scientific evidence indicates that entrainment is an effective method for inducing non-ordinary states of consciousness.[13]

Largely because of our hectic lives in modern society, it can be difficult to successfully entrain one's brain, in a single step, from a stressed to a deeply meditative state. For this reason, many mind machines come with pre-programmed sessions that take the user, in several, progressive steps, through a sequence of stimuli of different frequencies. Some of these sessions are even programmed to go as far as inducing a nap or sleep – both conducive to lucid dreaming, if one knows what one is doing – and they can be surprisingly effective at it. Initially at least, it may be a good idea to use these pre-programmed sessions, for they are often based on best-practices learned from what seems to work for most people. That said, we are all individuals with unique characteristics. Many mind machines therefore allow their users to program new, customized sessions themselves, with the aid of computer software. This way, you can construct your own sequence of stimuli to optimally take you from your regular state of consciousness to a non-ordinary one. It takes time to learn what works best *for you* and extensive trial and error may be required, with initially frustrating results. Nonetheless, this may be a case where patience and perseverance ultimately do pay off.

Some of the more advanced mind machines are equipped with special goggles capable of generating the so-called "Ganzfeld" effect.[14] The goggles generate a uniform, undifferentiated, featureless field of light that occupies practically the entire visual field of the user. Unable to pick any patterns out of the featureless visual stimulus, the brain switches off the signals from the eyes and starts amplifying internal neural signals instead, in a last-ditch attempt to look for visual cues. These purely internal signals, which would normally be overwhelmed by visual stimuli and remain under the threshold of explicit awareness, are now interpreted by the visual cortex as images. The result, as shown by psychologist Wolfgang Metzger in the 1930s, is a heightened propensity to visual "hallucinations." The question, of course, is whether these supposedly hallucinated images are actually real, valid impressions imprinted onto the brain by a non-local field of consciousness, albeit normally falling below the threshold of explicit awareness. Surprisingly, scientific analysis has indeed shown that such possibility is plausible.[15] If that is the case, then the Ganzfeld effect could be helpful in accessing valid knowledge otherwise unavailable to our five senses. A mind machine session that initially takes you, through an optimal sequence of different stimuli, from an ordinary to a non-ordinary state of consciousness, and then ends with a prolonged and silent Ganzfeld period, may produce highly rewarding results.

It should be noted that most mind machines expose the user to flashing lights and intense visual patterns. With some people, this can cause seizures.[16] It is prudent to always read the accompanying instructions and eventual contraindications before using any mind machine.

A mind machine is basically an externally-operating, wearable aid to meditation. There also exist internally-operating, consumable aids called *entheogens*. These are naturally-occurring, psychoactive substances used for the purpose of chemically inducing, or helping induce, a non-ordinary state of consciousness. They have been used by traditional cultures throughout history and across the world in religious, spiritual, and shamanic contexts. They have also been used as medicines, the effectiveness of such use having been carefully and extensively documented in two scholarly tomes – totaling 728 pages(!) – by Michael Winkelman and Thomas Roberts.[17] The traditional use of entheogens entails the consumption of plants or fungi that naturally contain the psychoactive compound. Here are some examples of entheogens: *ibogaine*, traditionally used in Africa, is a compound contained in the root of the Iboga plant (*Tabernanthe iboga*); *psilocybin* and *psilocin* are alkaloids contained in many different species of mushrooms and truffles traditionally consumed for religious and shamanic purposes, particularly in Central America; *Mescaline* is the active compound of the peyote cactus (*Lophophora williamsii*), legally used in religious rituals of Native American Indians in the USA; *DMT* is a psychoactive compound naturally present in the human body and in many species of plants. In South America, DMT has a history of traditional use as the main active component of, for instance, the ayahuasca brew – also called yagé, hoasca, and several other names – legally used as a sacrament by some churches in Brazil, as well as by indigenous shamans across the continent.

My limited literature review indicates overwhelmingly that entheogens, by and large, are not physically addictive. In fact, entheogens have been used precisely in the treatment of severe chemical dependencies like heroin, alcohol, and nicotine addiction.[18] Although most entheogens were made illegal in most countries starting with the psychedelic backlash of the late 1960s – due largely to their chemical similarity with the synthetic drug LSD (lysergic acid diethylamide) – at the time this book was written there appeared to be countries, jurisdictions, and circumstances in the world in which each of the entheogens mentioned above could be consumed legally. Depending on where one lives and on which entheogen one wants to experiment with, reaching these jurisdictions may require long-distance and difficult travel. This is often discouraging. Therefore, let me state unequivocally here that I do not recommend nor in any way encourage the breaking of the law of the land, not even in cases where scientific studies may contradict the premises of this law. Moreover, even where the consumption of an entheogen is entirely legal, it is my view that legality is no substitute for abundant caution, good judgment, and responsibility when one is considering the eventual use of these powerful substances.

Terence McKenna, an expert in both the phenomenology and pharmacology of entheogens, has suggested that the trypta-mines are the most effective psychoactive compounds for accessing knowledge "that seemed not to be drawn from the personal history of the individual or even from the collective human experience."[19] He referred to the source of this knowledge as the "Logos."[20] Of the list of entheogens mentioned above, the tryptamines are psilocybin, psilocin, and DMT. In the human body, psilocybin is quickly metabolized into psilocin, which is the compound actually responsible for the awareness expansion effects. Therefore, our short list of tryptamines consists simply of psilocin and DMT. Now, psilocin is 4-hydroxy-dimethyltryptamine, while DMT is N,N-dimethyltrypt-amine. Both are chemically very similar to serotonin, which is 5-hydroxytryptamine. Serotonin is an important neurotransmitter in the human nervous system. It is thus thought that tryptamine entheogens perturb ordinary brain function by fitting into the serotonin receptors of brain cells. In a way, tryptamine entheogens are believed to mimic the action of serotonin in the brain, mediating thought and perception like serotonin does, though obviously with different effects. The specific mechanisms by means of which this induces transcendent experiences are not understood, for the mechanisms of consciousness are themselves not understood. Nonetheless, it is a speculative possibility that tryptamine entheogens, when acting in lieu of serotonin, enable a bypass of certain evolved filtering mechanisms of the brain.

Since the 1990s, scientific studies inspired by the potentially beneficial psychological effects of tryptamine entheogens have resumed. The first of these studies was that carried out by Rick Strassman, M.D., at the University of New Mexico's School of Medicine. Dr. Strassman administered DMT to sixty healthy human volunteers and thoroughly measured both their physiological and psychological responses. He was surprised with the intense influx of peculiar impressions reported by his volunteers. As he wrote, the volunteers "unquestionably had some of the most intense, unusual, and unexpected experiences of their lives. [DMT] thrust research subjects into themselves, out of their bodies, and through various planes of reality."[21] Volunteers' reports forced Dr. Strassman to reconsider his reductionist model of the visionary experience. As he wrote, "it is almost inconceivable that a chemical as simple as DMT could provide access to such an amazingly varied array of experiences."[22] He went on to acknowledge the possibility that the impressions received by his volunteers may have indeed come, somehow, from outside their heads and may have been, at some level, ontologically valid – that is, real. In a later work, Dr. Strassman went on to write what, in my view, is a lucid and responsible orientation for those interested in tryptamine entheogens.[23]

In 2006, another study of tryptamine effects, this time at the world-renowned Johns Hopkins' Medical School, investigated the efficacy of psilocybin – that is, of psilocin – in treating depression and death anxiety in cancer patients. In their conclusions, the researchers wrote that "psilocybin, when administered under comfortable, structured, interpersonally supported conditions to volunteers who reported regular participation in religious or spiritual activities, occasioned experiences which had marked similarities to classic mystical experiences and which were rated by volunteers as having substantial personal meaning and spiritual significance. Furthermore, the volunteers attributed to the experience sustained positive changes in attitudes and behavior that were consistent with changes rated by friends and family."[24]

The consumption of entheogens can potentially have undesirable side-effects like nausea, vomiting, diarrhea, accelerated heart rate, elevated blood pressure, anxiety attacks, dissociation, temporary psychosis, etc. Depending on one's physical and psychological predispositions, existing medical conditions, and the manner and circumstances of consumption, these side-effects can become dangerous and even life-threatening. Possession and consumption of most entheogens is also illegal in most jurisdictions, carrying severe penalties. Therefore, more so than for any other technology of awareness expansion discussed here, caution and extensive background research are indispensible before anyone should even consider experimenting with entheogens.[25]

Such undesirable facts and circumstances have motivated psychiatrist Stanislav Grof, M.D., Ph.D., together with his wife, to develop a method that could reproduce the non-ordinary states of consciousness induced by entheogens, but without the consumption of the substances themselves. The result of this work is now known as "Holotropic Breathwork,"[26] a technique involving group work, intensified breathing, listening to evocative music, a form of focused bodywork, and the drawing of mandalas. The main causal element in the efficacy of Holotropic Breathwork seems to be the intensified breathing, or voluntary hyperventilation. Hyperventilation is known to raise the alkalinity level of the blood and cause constriction of blood vessels in the brain. This, naturally, perturbs ordinary brain function and is a reason why lightheadedness and fainting are sometimes observed in association with hyperventilation. Interestingly, in an article published in the Journal of Alternative and Complementary Medicine, it has been suggested that Holotropic Breathwork may reduce the efficacy of certain brain filters, "resulting in disinhibition of previously avoided or 'suppressed' internal stimuli."[27] Holotropic Breathwork, like all technologies discussed here, has contraindications and potential side-effects, and should be done under qualified supervision.

There are many other techniques of awareness expansion. Ancient Greeks used to descend into dark caves seeking the sensory deprivation that elicited non-ordinary states of consciousness. Through these non-ordinary states they believed they could access the ultimate wisdom, or "the immortals' knowledge."[28] Sufi Dervishes of the Mevlevi order use a form of spinning dance that also induces a trance, by means of which they hope to reach the source of all perfection. In the Christian West, it has been known that religious experientialists and people of strong and authentic religious faith seem able to achieve gnosis through intense prayer and other forms of worship. Even hypnosis has been used as a technique for inducing mystical trances.[29] There are just too many different technologies to mention here at any length. I hope the incomplete list I have tried to compile serves as a starting point for further research by anyone interested in deepening his or her knowledge of the subject.

When an individual technique of awareness expansion is not effective or sufficient for the achievement of an unambiguous experience, some of the technologies described can, in principle, be combined for enhanced effect. Extra caution and conservatism are prudent in such cases, for the result may turn out to be more intense than one has bargained for. Different techniques, and different combinations, seem to work better for different people. I have known people who, after years of dedicated training and effort, believe to have never truly reached non-ordinary states of consciousness through meditation or visualization; others seem to succeed after the first or second attempt, to their own amazement and surprise, and the envy of their peers. Some people whom I shared my mind machine with have found it extraordinary; others have dismissed it as a nonsensical gizmo. It seems that there are no set rules for what works with each individual.

All the techniques discussed here aim at lowering certain attention barriers in the brain to enable the influx of knowledge being sought. But by doing precisely that, all of these techniques can potentially lower our defenses against our own hidden fears, frustrations, and all manner of buried, negative images, thought patterns, and pathological behaviors, making us temporarily vulnerable to them. Caution and good judgment are indicated.

Chapter 5

Before the experiments

The hypothesis I have set out to verify is whether, through the technologies of awareness expansion, one can access knowledge about reality not previously recorded in, or misleadingly generated by, the brain. If such a hypothesis is correct, my goal is then to pursue a careful exploration of mind through expanded states of awareness, so to learn as much as possible about potential underlying aspects of nature not amenable to objective investigation. Success did not come easily: many failures and discouragement preceded its first foreshadowing signs. For long periods of time, I was convinced that either I was incapable of achieving a transcendent experience or such experiences were mere mirages. My instinctive skepticism very nearly overshadowed my innate curiosity and led me to dismiss the whole enterprise with a condescending hand wave. But once the first subtle hints began to trickle in that something different was going on, my cynicism waned a little. I began identifying the changes in technique and attitude that seemed to lead me in the right directions. From that point on, the learning curve accelerated quickly. This I attribute not only to the improvements in the technique itself, but also to a new and heartfelt intuition that success was tangible and not just an abstraction.

Before I report on the results of the experiments, I want to leave on record what my thoughts and expectations were *before* I carried out these experiments. I believe it to be methodologically sound, when it comes to subjective exploration, to contrast original expectations with achieved results in attempting to determine the validity of such results. The lines below have been written in a kind of diary long, long before the idea of writing this book ever took shape in my mind. Short of translating some of its segments from the language in which they were originally written, and of some changes aimed at improving its structure and continuity, the text below faithfully reflects its original content and tone.

"It is hard to imagine how it feels to go through an experience that most people who have undergone it describe, first and foremost, as *in*describable. I have spent a significant amount of time pouring through literally hundreds of reports from people who claimed to have had significant transcendent experiences, all in an attempt to form a reasonably accurate mental picture of what could be expected if and when I am capable of undergoing one such experience myself. But I have failed in that endeavor. If anything, despite the undeniable and overwhelming consistency of *themes*, the subjective language and variety of incongruent metaphors used by those firsthand witnesses wonder but confuse. One can perhaps only vaguely intuit the depth and breadth of what they have undergone. Indeed, there is a vague, ephemeral, but very intriguing ring of familiarity to some of the reports, at least for me; a familiarity more like the memory of a distant dream than something that one can put a finger on. As a memory, it feels almost alien, as if I were recalling something that happened to someone else.

"An overwhelming theme conveyed by most people whose reports I have read is a profound change of perspective. It is, as far as I could understand, as though the entire world took on a new meaning. The things, the people, the phenomena, are all still materially identifiable as what they were before, but one's understanding of their true nature changes retroactively. Apparently, it is as if you suddenly comprehended that the true nature of all things familiar to you has, *all along*, been very different from what you have always thought it to be. Many witnesses describe it as a form of awakening; a deeper understanding that bestows familiar reality with new meaning, while remaining consistent with its physical perception. This new interpretation is somehow believed to be much truer, much more real and authentic, than the one that preceded it. The earlier interpretation of reality is then seen as limited, equivocated, almost illusory; as a state of stupor or daze. The irony of this reverse symmetry is obvious.

"In struggling to visualize what that all may mean, I came up with a metaphor. I am the biological son of my parents, so the metaphor is a bit abstract even to me. Nonetheless, here it is: I tried to imagine how it would feel if, tomorrow, someone whose integrity and reliability were beyond question, told me that I was adopted as a baby; that the people I have always believed to be my biological parents were not genetically related to me at all; that the place and circumstances of my birth, as I conceived of them, have *all along* only existed in my imagination; that the entire first year of my life was very, very different from what I have always thought it to have been; that I am, in a way, a different person from the one I believed to be. This is the kind of retroactive, perspective-changing realization that throws one's entire universe upside-down *without actually changing anything that is or has ever been in it*. All that is changed is the *mental model* one uses to perceive reality; that is, one's worldview. My understanding of the transcendent experience, as I write these words, entails this kind of profound shift in perspective. It entails a break with old mental models that reaches back in time and gives you a new understanding, a new and perhaps more direct and truer picture not only of what is but of what has been. And yet, this shift in perspective must remain entirely consistent with the physical perception of reality one has had all along.

"There is, I must confess, an element of anxiety associated with attempting a transcendent experience. It is not overwhelming, though. The sheer *curiosity* and, frankly, even the little dab of skepticism I confess to have about the whole thing, tend to bury this anxiety in the background. Nonetheless, it is there. After all, once one crosses a certain perception threshold, one is committed to the memories of the experience regardless of how perspective-changing or disturbing those may be. One cannot unlearn what will have been learned, and the new knowledge must somehow be integrated.

"Based on my research so far, the most potentially disturbing element of the transcendent experience seems to be the apparent dissolution of the ego. That is perceived by some – perhaps the more impressionable ones – as a death-like experience. It is my hope that, if there is anything to it at all, with careful preparation I will be able to deal effectively with the feeling of ego disso-lution and integrate it well after the experience. Nonetheless, this element is undeniably sobering and commands respect and caution about the entire thing.

"My key aspiration for the transcendent experience rests in the possibility of a *direct, model-free* understanding of the meaning and purpose of existence. From a more rational perspective, one of my main objectives is to analytically verify, to my own satisfaction, whether external knowledge can be imprinted onto my physical memory through a mechanism that, through a process of elimination, can be ascertained to bypass all known physical means. No orthodox, reductionist explanation of the transcendent experience could account for such an input of impressions."

Here my original diary entry ends. Reading it again now, I cannot help but consider those words somewhat naïve. My model of the transcendent experience seemed to entail, as its most transcendent elements, things still describable with language in the context of 3-dimensional space and linear time. I had no idea of what really was to come, and how much beyond my wildest expectations it turned out to be. Perhaps it was best that way.

In the next chapters, I will attempt to describe as accurately and completely as possible the most significant experiences I have had while in non-ordinary states of consciousness. However, one should bear in mind that such experiences often transcend the scope of language. Indeed, all languages are based on tacit, prior sharing of experiences and concepts. This way, if I use the word "sad" you understand what I mean because you have had the experience of being sad before, and you know that that is what I am referring to. *The meaning of words is anchored on these shared experiences.* The problem with using language to describe a transcendent experience is that what one experiences may sometimes bear so little resemblance to anything else that precious little semantic anchoring exists. One is then left with precarious and imprecise metaphors to try and capture at least a smidgen of what has been perceived or understood. As I know now, *this fact may very well explain the apparent diversity and inconsistency of descriptions of the transcendent experience that one finds in the literature.* Each person interprets and describes the ineffable in his or her own idiosyncratic way, dressing it in the clothes and biases of his or her own worldview.

A transcendent experience is emotionally charged. Therefore, while I normally prefer to use sober, precise, and objective language in describing the results of any experiment, in this case I have allowed myself the use of liberal doses of metaphor and subjectivity. Indeed, there is no other way to appropriately describe an experience that is, by nature, subjective and largely beyond words. Any attempt to describe it soberly and objectively would be futile and defeat the purpose of description in the first place. That said, in later chapters I will attempt to return to a more balanced tone and, with more perspective on the experiences, carry out a balanced analysis and interpretation of their outcome.

In the next four chapters, the raw, unfiltered, subjective data representing the outcome of four experiments are described. Several other experiments have been carried out, with varying degrees of success, but these are the four most relevant ones from a philosophical point of view. While each report corresponds to one actual experiment, I sometimes add to the respective description a few related data elements that were in reality derived from other, similar, complementary experiments not worthy of reporting on their own. Each report was written a couple of days after the corresponding experiment was carried out, so to capture the associated impressions with the fidelity of a fresh memory, but also some minimum amount of perspective. Though I did edit out the more intensely personal parts, the respective texts are true to the experiences they describe. Finally, it may be useful to remember, while reading the next four chapters, that they were written well before all other parts of this book, including the present and preceding chapters.

Chapter 6

First experiment: Returning home from exile

Though I refer to what I will report here as my "first experiment," I had made earlier and partly successful attempts at
non-ordinary states of consciousness as part of my early
research and preparation. Those experiences were not philosophically relevant, so I have chosen not to discuss them here.
They were also ambiguous, light-weight experiences, which
probably fomented a slightly cavalier attitude in me regarding
future attempts. I know this only in hindsight, for my main
concern at the time of this experiment was to ensure that I
would go deeper than in previous occasions. Because of all the
schedules of life, appropriate opportunities to embark in such
experiments did not present themselves often. Therefore, I was
determined not to waste this chance with another mildly
curious, but philosophically trivial, result. This concern with
achieving a significant and unambiguous result, and the
eagerness associated with it, framed my mental attitude going
into the experiment. I was perhaps less respectful of the whole
process than I should have been. And ultimately, I paid a price
for it.

All the preparations completed and the process of subtle
consciousness shift well under way, I slowly began noticing a
change in perception. These early stages are very curious and
pleasant. You are fully aware of whom you are, of the circumstances around you, and you can reason just as well as in
ordinary states of consciousness. But there is such a lightness
associated to these early stages, such an effortless flow of
feelings, thoughts, and inner perceptions, that you feel relaxed

and, quite frankly, entertained with your own inner world. From my research, I knew that at some point it was important that I allow myself to become fully immersed in this stream of inner motion so a barrier could be crossed into the next state of consciousness. There, hopefully, something significant about the nature of reality would become cognizable. Still following a game-plan thoroughly researched and defined well in advance, I deliberately adopted an expectation of discovery, or learning; a visualization of a feeling, if you will; the feeling of under-standing something new shortly. This was an attempt to steer the general flow of events towards the outcome I desired.

In hindsight, there was something a lot more specific about my expectations, which I was not explicitly aware of at the time. Namely, deep inside me what I wanted, and expected, was to experience what mystics, shamans, religious experiencers, and psychologists throughout history have called "ego dissolution." I desired and expected to break free from my own sense of identity and again feel connected to the universe at large, as I once did as a child. As I understand now, I had two motivations for this desire that I had kept hidden from myself: first, I wanted to confirm, *through direct experience*, my own metaphysical position that consciousness, in its most fundamental and unfil-tered state, is boundless and unified; second, I wanted to experience freedom from my own ego, which I had identified as the source of all the negative and unpleasant feelings that haunted me. Little did I know then that I was about to learn a powerful, completely unexpected, exhilarating, *and* painful lesson about this.

Very subtly, my perceptions were shifting further. I began to drift, for what I believed was the first time in my adult life, into an inner world that felt strangely familiar. I was still aware of my body and circumstances. I could still feel the clothes touching my skin, my breath, and my heartbeat. But these slowly became remote sensations, as if I were aware of two parallel realities concurrently: an inner reality towards which I was gravitating with increasing speed, and an outer reality that I was not loosing connection with but which was becoming increasingly remote and abstract.

It is impossible to describe with language how subtly this transition happens. Let me just say that I was already deep into a peculiar inner reality for a long time, or at least for what felt to me like a long time, before I registered in awareness that an unfathomable shift had taken place. I guess I had expected, before the experiment, that this transition between states of consciousness would be immediately obvious. After all, how could anyone possibly descend into dreamland without noticing it? Yet, that is exactly the way it went. I know this sounds illogical, but here is what I think happens: during subjective exploration, one never completely loses the ability to reason. At least in my case, I was making constant use of my reasoning in order to try and interpret what I was experiencing and make mental notes for later use, once back to ordinary states of consciousness. For me, this was an *experiment* above all else: I was there to observe, interpret, and record. I believe one's continuing occupation with one's own reasoning provides a degree of continuity that smoothens out what would otherwise be a perhaps abrupt transition. Reasoning somehow grounds one's perceptions and distracts one's attention from the amazing change of context that consciousness undergoes.

So where exactly did I find myself once I realized a transition had taken place? This is the most interesting and unexpected part. My first realization was of how *absolutely familiar and recognizable* the experience seemed to be. It felt as if I had been in that "place of mind," on and off, all my existence. It felt like *the most familiar place* one can find oneself in; an overwhelming sense of returning to one's only true home. But then again, that could not be true: under rational analysis, there was an inescapably bizarre quality about the whole thing. It took me some mental processing to interpret what I was perceiving because I could not match it to any memory or circumstance of my life. Here is the best metaphor I have: *it was as if I were re-experiencing the inner life of myself as an infant,* perhaps a newborn. A much more outrageous explanation, which I somehow am unable to discard, is the possibility that I was re-experiencing a state of mind from *before* I was born or even conceived. But I do not want to touch on the implications of this, so let us stay with the infant interpretation. Mind you, I did not feel like I was an infant again. No. Instead, I felt as though I were *recalling,* with absolute and effortless clarity, what it might have felt like to be an infant. I was immersed in the inner life I might have had as a newborn.

I emphasize the terms "inner life" because it had nothing to do with perceptions of the objective world "out there." In fact, I had no recollection of any visual or auditory perception of external, objective things at all; not of my parents, not of my cradle, not of my room, nothing. That is the reason my association of the experience with my hypothetical inner life as an infant is but a metaphor: I do not have any concrete information to believe it besides the overwhelming feeling of primordial being.

Nonetheless, continuing on with the use of this metaphor, I could again perceive the abstract images and sounds that might have occupied my mind as an infant. Each of those would evoke powerful feelings. I remember constantly repeating to myself, mentally, after each image or sound would flash in my mind: "I remember that! And that! Wow, I remember *all* of it so clearly!" It was a growing and overwhelming feeling of unequivocal familiarity, remembrance, and comeback. It felt like finally coming home to the *source* of my own self; to the very thing that it truly means to be myself, after a long time in exile; an exile so long that I had even forgotten where I was from; in fact, so long that I had even forgotten that I even came from somewhere else originally. I felt absolutely safe, without a care or responsibility in the world. I had no worries, doubts, regrets, frustrations, ambitions, goals, guilt, nothing. I was experiencing a pure state of contentment that required nothing from the outside. The part of my conscious self that was still furiously reasoning about all this thought of my parents. I reasoned that I was probably reliving the feelings of being protected and taken care of by them. While I must acknowledge now that this is indeed the simplest explanation for how I felt, my reaction to this reasoning *while in the experiment* was different. Indeed, during the experiment my feeling was that I was in the presence of a protective, nurturing force, but I could not associate that force with anything or anyone outside of me. In a way, it felt as though an aspect of me were nurturing and protective of another aspect of myself; as if subject and object were, somehow, as illogical as it strikes me to be as I write these words, *the same thing*; as if experienc*er* and experience were one.

The images flashing in my mind were coherent and geometrical in nature. Most were somewhat related to the concentric, symmetric, recursive mandalas drawn in sand by Tibetan monks (see Figure 1), but more abstract and multidimensional. It was as though I could see the mandalas, with my mind's eye, only a few centimeters in front of me. Their patterns would evolve and self-transform in intricate and indescribable ways. It occurred to me that Tibetan mandalas were not mere symbols of abstract spiritual concepts, but that the monks could *actually see* the mandalas while in deeply meditative states! That was a surprise to me. Carl Jung considered mandalas to be the "psychic centre of the personality not to be identified with the ego,"[1] but it had never occurred to me that such symbolism could be so literal. Other images were more fluidic in nature, akin to fractal flames (see Figure 2). Sounds also accompanied this curious display of evolving geometric forms. They were more like simple, subtle rhythms than melodies. Somehow my perception was that these rhythms fitted perfectly with the

Figure 1. An example of a Tibetan mandala.

Figure 2. A computer-generated fractal flame.

images and, together, they were even more evocative of the abstract inner feelings of the infant I once was, or of whatever primordial form I once had. *Those images and sounds were the sensory keys for opening the doors to my original, earliest inner life.* The reason I am making an effort to describe these elusive mental images, and the philosophical significance I see in them, will become apparent later.

The sense of my own identity was intact. In fact, it was expanded in a way, as if I actually were more than I thought before. I felt emotional at this stage: the emotion of being re-united with a very important part of me that I had left behind very long ago and then forgotten about. In what strikes me now as a cognitively dissonant perception, but which during the experiment felt perfectly reasonable, I was able to concurrently recognize that previously forgotten part of me both as myself *and* as someone separate from me. I felt the deepest and sincerest affection for that "infant" I had just re-encountered after a lifetime, and who was profoundly meaningful, significant, and important to me.

As the mandala-like imagery seemingly pacing and coordinating the entire experience evolved and self-transformed, new inner feelings were evoked. It felt as though I were unfolding into multiple versions of myself, in a smooth flow of rhythm and coherence. The sounds were now more like a sound track, which amplified the emotional significance of the experience like a score does to a movie. At this point, my perception of linear time went out the window. As the images unfolded, I felt my consciousness move in and out of the inner life I had at different times. Yet, that did not happen in a linear sequence, but rather as if the phonograph needle could move to random locations of the record of my inner life. Multiple tracks could be played at once, forward or backward, and at different speeds.

While experiencing all this, I thought to myself how utterly personal the whole experience was. I had not expected it and I know now that I was not prepared for it. I had expected – or rather hoped for – a stream of knowledge not normally accessible to ordinary states of consciousness, but which were still applicable to an interpretation of reality in general. Instead, I got something that was meaningful solely to my own self. This confused me. I went into the experiment with the intent to observe and analyze impartially, but the experience hit me in such an inescapably personal manner that any attempt at impartiality felt hopeless. The experience was not only about me; *the experience was me*. Whatever distance I might have intended to maintain between myself and what I was observing was quickly smashed to nothingness.

I had unfolded into different versions of myself, which were now part of a stream of images and feelings I was immersed in and swimming through. But then these different "versions" of me began to merge back into what I could only describe as a kind of felt core of my identity. I felt a re-integration of all those forgotten personalities. At each re-integration step, I felt a growing sense of integrality: as though I were reattaching the pieces of myself that fell off and were left behind on the road of my existence through linear time. A deep feeling of joy and gratitude filled me.

As I mentioned earlier, before the experiment I had the unacknowledged desire to dissolve my own sense of identity and separateness. *Yet, I was getting the exact opposite of all that.* I was being reminded of the tremendous evocative power of my own identity. I was being brought back to the original, forgotten source and core of that identity. I was swimming, completely immersed, in a sea of *me*. I was being shown how important it was to recover the lost pieces of myself so to become an integral entity again. I was being shown how much I actually cared about these aspects of myself that I had carelessly and cavalierly allowed to fall off along the way. Yet none of it seemed to carry with it any of the notions of egoism, arrogance, self-centeredness, fear, and pettiness that I tended to associate with the ego. *There was something important, fundamental indeed, about the sense of self, the "I," that transcended the notion of the ego. I had been mixing these things up until that point.*

At this time in the experience, a clear and coherent message arose in a flash in my conscious mind, already fully formed as it came, and in my own voice: *"before you accomplish anything else, you must first be whole."* Upon cognizing this message, my mental attitude turned into one of sobriety and pensiveness. How naïve I had been. My obsessive search for the simplest explanation had led me to miss something crucial not only about reality, but about myself: *there is something fundamental to being an individualized, conscious entity that transcends the mere notion of the ego constructed by the physical brain as a survival tool. There must be a level of reality where consciousness is individualized in a focal point, an "I," yet independently of the brain.* The logic, or perhaps the lack thereof, of these statements aside, they felt to me as self-evident truths during the experiment.

Throughout all this, I still had that profound sense of safety and belonging that had absorbed me early in the experiment. Having been forced by this latest insight to put the value of my own rationality in perspective, my enthusiasm for reasoning waned. I became a lot more contemplative as opposed to inquisitive. I allowed myself to drift into the flow of those feelings of safety and belonging, without active reasoning or thought, for a period of time that I cannot estimate. I can just say that, at some point, my entire perception of the self in the context of a culture, of a society, of a name, and of a life in linear time, all vanished. I guess that, upon giving up my efforts to reason, which had been anchoring my experience up until that point, I drifted into yet another, yet more transcendent state of consciousness. I believe *that* is what people have called "ego dissolution." I had drifted into a state of pure, context-free awareness and I had not even noticed it as it was happening. My consciousness still had a focal point; that is, there was still an "I," but one freed from all life- and identity-related contextual baggage. There was no sense of fear, panic, or imminent death, as many have described. Instead, what happened was a smooth and seamless transition into an experience of pure being, in which I either had no perceptions, thoughts, or impressions, or I do not remember any of it. Language completely breaks down here, but I will try to convey the only articulation I seem to have brought back from this part of the experience: I was not dead, but I was not alive either. There was no life as we normally understand it. As such, one is not alive in that state. The differences between life and death, past and future, and many other polarities, all become very diffused and slippery. There is an amoral quality of emptiness to it, yet there is focalized consciousness experiencing it. Think of the Cheshire cat's grin in "Alice's Adventures in Wonderland:" the grin stays behind after the cat itself slowly disappears. This is how it feels in that state: the Cheshire cat of life and the ego slowly disappears, leaving behind the grin of pure conscious experience in the form of a recognizable "I." To me, there was nothing unpleasant or scary about being in that state of consciousness. I just *was*.

Now what really hits you is the *coming back*. If the going was smooth and pleasant, the coming back was like a steamroller running over me. It started with flashes of what I now can recognize as images of my life in the present time but which, during the experience, had an unfathomable sense of abstractness and remoteness to them; like a vague, distant, and mostly forgotten dream. They were like images of someone else's life when that someone else is, metaphorically, an alien living in a very peculiar, flat, limited, claustrophobic, and utterly weird world with strange and oppressive laws of physics. I saw flashes of the alien sitting in a funny metal box, holding and manipulating a strange circular device whose movements seemed somehow to be magically synchronized to the movements of the metal box as a whole. I then saw flashes of the alien looking at a strange, flat diagram divided into seven blocks, paying special attention to one of the blocks – the rightmost one. That block had particular meaning to the alien, for it corresponded to the segment of the alien's life that was most present in his awareness. The block had little symbols in it: "s u n d a y." It then dawned on me that the entire life of the alien was somehow ruled by that insignificant little diagram. How oppressive and appalling! The alien appeared to be confused, wandering through strange and bizarre places, ever farther from the source of warmth and nurturing that he needed to survive. He seemed vulnerable and exposed, loaded with a heavy, almost unbearable sense of responsibility, and having to perform strange, seemingly unnatural tasks to protect whatever degree of comfort and reassurance he could still eke out of his bizarre existence. And then came the ominous realization that smashes you: "*that*, my friend, is not an alien..."

From here on, the descent into life, identity, and linear time was a slow excursion into anguish. A deep sense of disorientation accompanies the return to ordinary consciousness before the ego fully reconstitutes itself. For a time, I was not quite sure about who or what I was, where I lived, or what I did. The sheer concepts of life, time, and geographical location had to be slowly remembered. All of this probably transpired in seconds, but it felt much longer. As I finally begun to reconstitute my ego and regain some composure, I crash-landed onto the memories of the less desirable elements of my life. Indeed, I learned that, while recovering one's ego provides welcome relief from the disorientation of the return, *along with one's ego come one's ghosts.* Have you ever had the experience of waking up immediately after a blissful, light, carefree dream, just to remember the bummers of your life? In those initial moments of wakefulness, when your defenses are still down and you have grown accustomed to the lightness of your dream, the bummers of your life jump out at you with a vengeance; until you finally manage to file them back into the mental drawers that keep them in check. The specifics of my experience re-encountering my private bummers are philosophically irrelevant, so I will spare you the details. All that is worth mentioning is that it was hard. Yet, in a way, it was a learning experience too. Through it, I became a lot more aware of the fears, frustrations, and machinations lurking in obfuscated layers of my own mind.

Something else I noticed is that, for a couple of days after the experiment, life and consensus reality took on an abstract, almost surreal quality. Living life felt like watching a kind of 3D full-immersion movie; there was such remoteness to everything around me. Deep inside, it felt as though what we call "reality" were not quite real; as if, in a way, my body were indeed a kind of remote-controlled alien living in a funny, low-dimensional, peculiar, virtual reality. This was a very palpable, very personal, and very sincere impression, not a theoretical abstraction. As I write these words, four days after the experiment, that feeling is almost entirely gone, just a subtle echo of it still ringing in my mind. Yet, I remain intrigued by it in a way that my rationality and skepticism cannot completely shake off.

Thinking about all this in these last four days, I realized that the frustration and fear associated to the bummers of my life exist only in my ego. The self seems to unfold into multiple manifestations at different levels. One level is a transcendent sense of "I'ness," so pure and unaltered by the models and filters of the physical brain that it seems to exist intact, in its full form, even when one is still a newborn. Another is the ego, molded by brain processes in order to improve the primate's chances of survival through desire and fear. These two manifestations of the self are different. *There is such a thing as a transcendent "I," and one does not need to destroy one's own identity in order to free oneself from the ego.*

The three different phases of the experiment – namely, the

blissfulness of the "infant," the non-life of the "egoless focal point of consciousness," and the oppression and sorrows of the time- and identity-bound "alien" – were like a sequence of "lessons." I have been shown that there exists a transcendent self, beyond the ego, who is very dear and important to me. I have then been shown that this transcendent self can penetrate a realm perhaps beyond the experience of life. *Consciousness, therefore, seems to precede life ontologically, not the other way around.* In other words, instead of life being a necessary condition for consciousness, perhaps consciousness is a necessary condition for life. This inversion of the direction of causality would remain entirely consistent with the correlation between life and consciousness that we seem to observe in ourselves and others. Finally, I have been given a very visceral demonstration of what the ego really is; a visceral demonstration of all the pain, sorrow, and fear that the ego holds on to and carries around with it.

If I carefully and critically consider the entirety of my experience, I must acknowledge that most of its aspects could, at least in principle, be explained by orthodox reductionist psychology. Indeed, one could imagine that I simply remembered inner feelings from long ago, but which were all along stored in my brain. One could also argue that the dissolution of the ego and of the sense of time that I experienced later in the experiment were mere artifacts of a self-inflicted dissociative process. Strictly speaking, the experiment did not yield enough evidence to *categorically* invalidate a reductionist explanation of its phenomenality. That said, the experiment did produce two pieces of evidence that seem *difficult* to place in an orthodox, materialist framework. The first is the direct experience of a focused, transcendent self, beyond the ego and the experience of life. As for the second, it took me two days of thinking about my experience to even notice the significance of it, for initially it had escaped me completely: *Why would mandala-like, evolving geometric figures be associated with, and evoke, memories of my primordial inner life?* The link between those images and my earliest sense of identity felt so obvious, so self-evident, and so natural to me, that I could not immediately see the screaming logical gap here: *If those images were memories, where did those memories come from to begin with?* If those were infant memories, where or how did I acquire memories of unfolding mandalas as a newborn? I certainly could not have seen those images with my physical eyes as an infant.

A possible orthodox explanation could be that these images were correctly remembered by me during the experience, but they were originally generated by my own brain in the past: infant imagination. This explanation, however, seems even more fantastic than the phenomenon it purports to explain. It is hard to believe that the temporal and spatial coherence of evolving, recursive geometric figures could have been spontaneously imagined by an immature physical brain. Indeed, when we imagine things as adults we use a lot of perceptual material accumulated with our physical senses in the course of our lives: sights, sounds, symbols, concepts, events, etc. An infant would have very little, if any, raw material to construct such intricate, evolving inner worlds.

Alternatively, one could argue that the mandala-like patterns were not infant memories, but were simply constructed by my brain *during* the experience. After all, my adult brain should be capable of imagining such sophisticated imagery. Beyond that, I could have simply fantasized the association between the patterns and infant memories, the association itself being false. While I cannot discard the possibility of this explanation being valid, here comes the value of a first-person investigation: as the person who had the experience directly, this explanation seems to me to lack sufficient explanatory power. Indeed, my recognition of the mandala-like images as the memories of a primordial inner life was overwhelming. If I accept so easily that this conviction is false, then it follows logically that I may have

59

to throw into doubt most other conclusions I hold to be true about reality. Therefore, if I am to continue with these experiments in a thoughtful manner, I must accept the knowledge derived from direct personal experience at least as valid hypotheses, even if that knowledge cannot be objectively proven to be correct. This means that, though I cannot try to convince others of the validity of the data – they would have to have their own direct experience of it – it is entirely legitimate that I base my own thoughts and speculations on that data. And then, I must find a logical framework to place and integrate those experiences.

Chapter 7

Second experiment: A lonely child king

As I crossed the threshold from consensus reality into a non-ordinary state of consciousness, the recognition of the transition was now easier. It is impossible to describe what it feels like with a sufficient degree of accuracy. One is forever confined to precarious metaphors in such cases. Nonetheless, *during the experience*, it all feels very familiar, normal, and trivial even. It is only now, as I write these words from a difficult recollection of what I experienced, that my regular thought patterns inform me of how extraordinary and difficult to explain the whole thing actually was. Image metaphors are the best I can come up with to convey the perceptual gestalt of the experience. In the context of this metaphor, I could say that I saw, with my mind's eye, beautiful spherical forms. They were akin to "Christmas balls" decorated with dazzling, dynamic and evolving, mandala-like geometric patterns (see Figure 3). Sometimes, these mandala patterns would protrude out of the smooth surfaces of the spheres, creating rich bas-reliefs and textures. Other times, the spheres would collide and geometric patterns would seem to come altogether loose from them, like debris spinning madly in the ether. The overall aspect of these loose, sparkling, spinning geometric forms was reminiscent of some abstract paintings by Wassily Kandinsky (see Figure 4). Yet, despite the obvious strangeness of it all from the point of view of an ordinary state of consciousness, it all felt trivially familiar; in fact, unambiguously so. *I knew this place intimately.*

It then dawned on me: *this* is where I was before, in my previous experiment. *These* were the mandala-like patterns I tried to describe earlier, except that now they were not "right

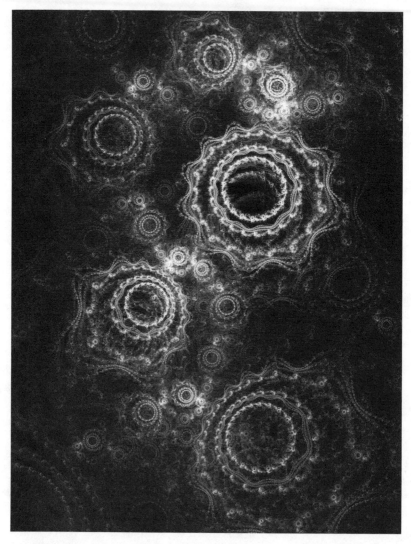

Figure 3. Computer art resembling the mandala-decorated "Christmas balls" of inner space.

Figure 4. "Kandinsky Scintilla," an interpretation by Natalia Vorontsova.

before my eyes" anymore. I had somehow "stepped back," gained more perspective, and could now more effectively perceive this "place in the mind" as a whole, as opposed to only close-up details.

This realization somehow enabled me to frame my perceptions and better make sense of the experience. The "place" was vast, deep, yet it had boundaries, like a large domed chamber. In this chamber, the "Christmas balls" floated around like planets in a star system, with spinning geometric forms detaching from them irregularly like glittering "Kandinsky scintillae." Despite the vastness of it, somehow everything within this place felt as though it was comfortably within my reach; as if I could wrap my arms around the entire place and embrace it in its totality. This was definitely *not* open space. In fact, there was a sense of this chamber being "underground," or inside some kind of solid superstructure of sorts, though I cannot point out anything specific that could have justified this impression.

There was an explanation that seemed to accommodate all these apparent contradictions: this place was buried inside me. *I* was the "superstructure" referred to above, or the "ground" where this chamber was buried. Though the place was vast, everything within it was easily within my reach because it was all in me. Indeed, this interpretation also explained why the experience was so familiar, self-evident, and non-mysterious to me at the time. *Naturally, if such explanation is correct, it requires a non-trivial redefinition of one's own self in order to accommodate so much phenomenality within the boundaries of that self.*

There was no doubt: I was back to the place where I had been during my last experiment. Last time it was different though: then, I felt as though I was back home for the first time after a long, long absence. The re-encounter with that place was special then, like a recovery of lost parts of me; like going back to one's hometown after a lifetime of exile. But now it was a different story. After all, I had just been there. The novelty factor was gone, and disappointment took over. I thought: "I set out to explore the unknown, learn new things, but instead I am back to the limit case of the known and familiar."

A wave of disappointment and skepticism about the potential novelty value of this experiment began to rise. I had to make a conscious effort to keep these feelings under control for I knew, from failures in the past, how delicate non-ordinary states of consciousness were and how precarious it was to hold on to them. Sometimes, even the slightest distraction would send me crashing down, back to consensus reality and regular perception. I succeeded in remaining in the experience, but I never really managed to escape the feeling of disappointment throughout. In fact, the feeling turned into light-hearted sarcasm, coming to dominate the experience, as I will describe below.

In my efforts to remain focused, I tried to pay closer attention to the situation. How exactly did things work in this mental place? Was there a kind of "physics" regulating its phenomenality? The moment these questions were posed, answers seemed to just pop into my mind. Yet this did not surprise me at all. As a matter of fact, it seemed that there was no other way things could work in this place: here, questions and answers just came always together. And here is the answer I got: *I was the fashioner of the reality of this space.* Its laws of physics were what I determined them to be. Everything in this chamber emanated from me and, therefore, was part of me in movement. The hovering spheres, like toy planets and stars in the space of this mental "inner theater," were emanations of my own mind; a kind of little proto-universe of my own.

Just as before, I felt like a child in this place; an almighty but lonely child; a child king left alone in a castle filled with spectacular toys and yet swimming in an agonizing sea of tediousness. I craved for *company* and *novelty.*

This metaphor of a child locked up in a toy room is appropriate in more ways than one. Indeed, there was a circus-like quality to this inner theater of mind. The general feeling associated, for example, with the "Kandinsky scintillae," as they spun madly in the ether, was one of absurdity. Though self-evidently emanating from me, in a way everything here had certain autonomy of its own, like archetypical automata embodying a form of proto-consciousness. But I was the sole entity in this place endowed with the power of intentionality. I missed having *someone else* to interact with.

It felt as if I had been alone in that place, on and off, for the longest of times. Because of that, regardless of how rich the environment of inner theater clearly was, I was so blasé about it all that my sole interest was to break out of it. The silliness of this quasi-autonomous circus spectacle was frustrating. Everything was so senseless that it ended up being... funny!

My initial frustration had now turned into a light-hearted, sarcastic acceptance of the situation; a kind of surrender to what is. You see, all these silly little geometric patterns spinning and drifting around my mind were utterly pointless. Yet, *that* is what made the whole thing amusing. I thought of some old Monty Python sketches and the way they were funny precisely because of their pointlessness and senselessness. It is the very hopelessness of the joke that is humorous in a self-defeating manner. Perhaps the same applies to some aspects of our lives in consensus reality... perhaps our inability to find closure should rather be a reason for good humor, as opposed to despair...

Part of me made an effort to understand just *why* this inner world seemed so pointless. Why did it seem so inconsequential? As usual in this place, the moment the question was formulated, it was accompanied by its answer: "it is inconsequential because it is all in your imagination." That made absolute sense. I already knew that *everything in this place, this inner theater of mind, was an unfolding of aspects of my inner self. Well, that is the very definition of "imagination,"* it seemed to me. Yet, in ordinary states of consciousness, we associate a kind on non-reality to the products of the imagination. Something is said to be "imaginary" when it is conceived but *not* realized. Well, such separation between conception and realization – between real and imaginary – did not seem to exist or to make any sense in the inner theater of mind. Not because nothing there was real, but precisely because *everything was as real as anything can possibly be.* In there, "real" and "imaginary" overlapped completely. They were entirely equivalent and interchangeable concepts. Saying that something was "imaginary," according to my cognition machinery during the experience, was the same as saying that it was "real," and vice-versa. *Conceiving was realizing. There was just imagination and it was very real.*

As one retains the ability to reason during the experience, I pondered about the "solid and enduring reality" of the lives we live under ordinary states of consciousness. I concluded immediately that that too, was imaginary; and yet no less solid, enduring, or real because of it. Later on, talking about my experience with my wife, an idea came to me already fully-formed. Perhaps the reality of the inner theater is just as imaginary as consensus reality, with one difference: in one's own inner theater the imagination is free to compose reality without external constraints, while *in consensus reality synchronization emerges across the imaginations of multiple conscious entities, so to form a coherent shared picture. The constraints entailed by such emergent synchronization may be what we call the laws of physics.* Perhaps the apparently fixed mechanisms of nature are merely an epiphenomenon; an emergent property of the sympathetic harmonization of different imaginations, imagination itself being the true primary substance of reality. Perhaps the laws of physics can themselves be reduced to a fundamental metaphysics of psyche. This is a heretical idea as far as science is concerned, but ironically so in the way it turns reduction, the prime canon of scientific thinking, against the basic axioms of science itself.

At some point, it dawned on me how preposterous my own expectations about exploring non-ordinary states of consciousness seemed to be. I was planning on exploring "majestic dimensions," learning about the "true and immutable nature of reality" and, perhaps, even experiencing "unified consciousness with all beings." How naïve of me! You see, *during the experience* there was nothing "transcendental," "mysterious," or "unknown" about what I was experiencing. *It was just the way things had always been.* I was just back to that place I had been in forever, surrounded by the pointlessness of the unfolding of aspects of my own mind. I heard myself say: "You are just back home my friend, and there is nothing greatly transcendent about it. Disappointed, are you?" It is curious how unceremoniously some brutal truths seem to be presented to you in inner theater. One should not go there expecting etiquette.

It gets better...

I suddenly remembered, to my utter amusement, that I had machinations about coming up with metaphysical models of reality based on my experiences. It is hard to describe how ludicrous this proposition seemed to me at that point. I could not help but chuckle at the image it evoked: as funny a caricature as that of a hamster busily plotting to build a rocket and go to the moon. How did I dare think that I could ever understand the underlying structure of reality sufficiently to model it? It was intuitively clear to me then that our condition as human beings is intrinsically associated with mystery, and that we must accept to live without closure. What I was planning to model was unknowable to a limited entity like me.

At this point of the experiment a thought was beginning to take hold on me: "I *can* get out of this tedious inner theater and return to something called life." Yes, I could just go back to my ordinary state of consciousness, back to consensus reality, and there would be *other people, other conscious entities* for me to interact with. I would not be alone anymore. There would be other things beyond my own unfolding aspects: *unknown things for me to explore, learn about, and enjoy.* There would be nature, sunsets, oceans, forests, cities, *outer* space, science, philosophy, life stories, drama, thrills, and all those things to keep one engaged. What a warm feeling those thoughts brought me.

This longing for the return was in stark contrast to my previous experiment. Then, the return was very painful and disorienting. Inner theater had felt blissful back then. This time, it seemed lonely and tedious without measure. The anticipation of the return to normal life offered a perspective of freedom, re-engagement with unknowns, and communion with others. Part of me was rationalizing the situation and trying to linger a little longer in that place to learn a little more. But the return was now inevitable, and it came quickly. Back to life! It felt good. Consensus reality seemed to offer lots of opportunities for *experiencing new things,* and I was looking forward to it. I came back rested and refreshed, ready for a full and active day, just to have to accept the fact that it was already late at night and the world around me was asleep.

I found it ironic how, once again, the experiment seemed to follow a pattern: each segment of the inner experience seemed to be a kind of lesson, complementing the previous one and setting the stage for the next one. Most likely, this interpretation is just a projection of my own intellect struggling to make sense of what I have experienced. Whichever way, it intrigues me. In my previous experiment, I had an overwhelming sense of how important it was to stay connected to that place, that inner theater of mind, the source of all it means to be me, in order to be a complete version of myself. Following that first experience, I had difficulties returning to normal life. For many days, deep inside me, I dismissed normal existence as an oppressive game. Now, in this latest experiment, I was shown how lonely and tedious life in inner theater could also be if one had no other perspective. This way, the value of life in consensus reality became clear to me in a very pungent manner. Are these pieces of a jigsaw puzzle that I must slowly put together?

Here is what I thought might happen: if one is in a place where one's deepest feelings and imagination instantly turn into palpable, "externalized" reality, then the entire reality of that place works as an amplifying mirror of one's own mind. By being immersed in that reality, one is confronted with one's own weaknesses and limitations of understanding. In my first experiment, the first feeling I had upon coming into inner theater was a feeling of warmth and reassurance; a feeling of returning home. That initial feeling was then amplified and set the tone for much of the remainder of the experiment, helping me understand the value of that return, as well as the fact that I had neglected the integrity of my own self throughout my life. In this second experiment, my initial feeling upon coming into inner theater was one of disappointment: I wanted to explore something new, not return to the limit case of familiarity. This feeling then, again, set the tone for the rest of the experiment, helping me understand that it is not enough to live in warmth and protection in that place, and that consensus reality out here is *also* something to aspire to. So perhaps the pattern of "lessons" is indeed a reflection of the contents of my own mind, externalized and played out in front of me in at least as real a manner as consensus reality.

Something else I believe to have learned is this: in my original metaphysical model, discussed in "Rationalist Spirituality," I had motivated the need for the apparent fragmentation of a universal field of consciousness on the basis of logic and the concept of information. This way, consciousness fragmentation was necessary for the creation of an information playing field that would, in turn, allow the universe to become self-aware. As true as this logic may be, it does not provide any clue as for the *emotional* motivation behind the act of consciousness fragmentation. Indeed, this created a problem in my original metaphysical model: it required action without explicit foreknowledge of the potential consequences of such action. The problem is that it is hard to imagine that an entity would choose to take action without having an explicit idea of what this action could potentially lead to; *unless there was an emotional imperative that led to action*. After all, we know that people do jump into the unknown, risking life and limb, when the status quo is emotionally unacceptable. It is precisely an idea about the emotional imperative behind consciousness fragmentation that I derived from this latest experiment: *the emotional imperative to overcome loneliness and, frankly, tedium*. I can now very clearly intuit the unfathomable forces this emotional imperative could have put in motion in a distant cosmological past.

From a rational perspective, one thing strikes me in this experiment: the consistency of what I now recognize as my "inner theater." It feels like a "place," though not quite a physical place the way we normally understand it. Rather, *it is a "place" because of the unique and ineffable emotional and perceptual qualities intrinsically and consistently associated with being there in awareness*. Nonetheless, based on my direct experience of it, I cannot help but make the conjecture that such place may be a coherent segment of the space-time fabric. Moreover, I seem to be consistently able to return to it and each time it is overwhelmingly recognizable as the *same* place. This quality of *repeatability*, so valued in science, seems to suggest that such place is not simply a random delusion. I am perfectly aware of how improbable a claim this is from a third-person perspective, but there is nothing I can do about how real it feels to me. I know I cannot, in good conscience, attempt to convince skeptics about it. Indeed, if I put myself in their shoes, I would dismiss the vey case I am suggesting here. What I can do is simply to share my thoughts and experiences, with honesty and integrity, and let people take from it whatever they may see fit, if anything. It is okay if the vast majority dismisses it as fantasy. I would too, had I not had the experiences myself.

Chapter 8

Third experiment: Gazing in awe at the backstage of reality

Frankly, I had modest expectations this time. I was bracing for the possibility that I would simply go back to inner theater for another repeat of the previous experiences, perhaps with some peripheral variations. However, I was in for what has turned out to be a perspective-changing experience; one I now consider the most significant I have ever had. But let us not rush things; let us cover it systematically and in chronological order.

The initial stages of the experience pretty much followed the previously established pattern. Upon crossing the threshold into a non-ordinary state of consciousness, I found myself once more in my own "private" inner theater, with the familiar and evocative mandala patterns and Kandinsky scintillae waiting for me. I stayed centered, carefully avoiding a drift into negative emotions that could set an undesirable tone for the rest of the experience. I visualized *the feeling* of learning something about the underlying nature of reality. This visualization was strong, for I very sincerely wished for greater understanding. Behind my visualization, perhaps hidden in obfuscated layers of my mind, there was a hint of disappointment that I had not yet had an unambiguous insight about reality, like many others had reported as a result of their subjective exploration practices.

From the familiar inner theater, I drifted further into that state of egolessness and non-life that I described earlier. This time, however, I recognized it as it was happening. I welcomed it and continued to actively try and keep my mind centered and disciplined as the experiment unfolded. Thankfully, I did not think about how difficult my previous return from egolessness had been.

My efforts to stay centered and lucid paid off. Shortly after reaching the state of egolessness, I broke through into new and uncharted territory. New, previously unseen images started flashing in my mind, accompanied but strange thoughts. I cannot recall what they were, but I remember wondering about what was going on. Some of the images seemed vaguely to resemble some weird form of visual art, akin to cubism. Whatever it was, it was very peculiar, as if I were tapping into a mind not my own; as if I were witnessing things, events, images, thoughts, and emotions that did not belong to me, or to any normal human being for that matter. It was not scary though: I was relaxed, open-minded and, frankly, very curious.

More than in previous experiments, I find it extraordinarily difficult this time to recall the details of the experience. Like a regular dream that one forgets seconds after waking up, this time the experience began fading fast, even before I was back to more ordinary states of consciousness. Still, I remember that, at some point in the experiment, I was saying repeatedly in thought: "I am trying, but I cannot understand it… I am trying…" Something was being displayed on the screen of my mind; something extraordinarily profound and complex, but I could not make sense of it. It was very, very hard to grasp, whatever it was.

The gestalt of the experience was that of a "better informed" alter ego of mine trying to convey something to his space-time-bound doppelganger. I had a hard time making sense of "his" message. Yet, very slowly, the entire situation started becoming clearer. At some point, I felt as though my supposed alter ego were metaphorically opening the dome of inner theater above my head – like the moving dome of an astronomical observatory – revealing a profound and unprecedented truth operating busily and inconspicuously just behind what had previously been the boundary of my perceptual universe.

74

What I then "saw" was indescribable. How inadequate words are. This... "thing" that was revealed... froze me to the spot. *It was a pattern.* Whatever doubt I might have harbored about whether these experiences truly entailed knowledge input from outside my brain evaporated: there was absolutely no way this thing, this unfathomable miracle of a pattern, could have come out of my primate head.

Suddenly it was completely clear. I could understand it! It was an unbelievably complex, yet self-explanatory evolution of concentric patterns growing out of concentric patterns; like self-generating, hyper-dimensional mandalas recursively blossoming, like flowers, out of the centers of previous hyper-dimensional mandalas, ad infinitum, but with a single point of origin from where it all emanated. This point of origin, this *Source* of it all, however, remained elusive: hidden behind the layers of wonders growing outwards from it. Somehow, the way new patterns unfolded and evolved was already entirely encoded in, and determined by, the very shapes, angles, and proportions entailed by previous patterns, so that no new primary information was ever added to the thing as it evolved. The entire story was already fully contained in it from the very beginning, and it was simply unpacking and manifesting itself in all its indescribable glory. It was a thing of startling power and beauty, yet put together with a level of sophistication and perfection that goes way beyond anything I could compare it to.

I was flabbergasted with how unambiguous this experience was. No fluffy and debatable impressions here; *this thing was there*. I could hardly believe it. Despite its sheer complexity, and unlike diagrams in a textbook – which require captions for their meaning to be made clear – this thing was entirely self-evident in its perfect harmony. Simply by "looking" at it I understood not only it, but its far-reaching implications as well. This was the answer to the question that haunted me my entire life: *this thing, this miraculous, hyper-dimensional, evolving pattern, was the defin-*

itive explanation to the underlying structure of reality. There was no doubt. This settled the question entirely. One simply needed to "look" at it with the mind's eye to know that this is how reality came to being; this is how nature was formed; this is what nature is; *this is what is behind everything.* There, in that pattern, in its wondrous shapes and features, in the angles, lengths, proportions, and relationships among its components, and in the way it evolved recursively as if re-birthing itself continuously, was the answer to everything. *The pattern was the answer.* At this point of the experience, there was no other reality to me but this jaw-dropping thing that was unfolding and revealing itself; physical body and life in linear time completely forgotten.

From the moment the metaphorical dome began to open, I felt thoughts in my mind that I did not recognize as my own. These were clearly and very gently articulated statements that popped seemingly out of nowhere: "You wanted to know... so here is how it is, you see? This is how it is..." These words came invested with a sense of calm and benevolence. "This is how it *all* is, you see?" spoke my supposed alter ego, borrowing my own voice.

There was a deep cognitive dissonance in my mind in the sense that, at the same time that the understanding of the pattern was absolutely clear to me, I was also incapable of articulating this understanding to myself in any intelligible manner. I remember thinking to myself in hopeless frustration: "How will I *ever* be able to share this with anybody else?" Here is how I interpreted what was taking place: the part of me that understood the pattern was instinctive consciousness, operating independently of the mental models in my brain. But only a lower-dimensional, fragmented, incomplete *projection* of that understanding could be imprinted onto my brain, perhaps through a process of wave function collapse.[1] Therefore, any attempt to articulate the understanding through mental symbol manipulations was doomed to fail.

Yet I could not stop trying. My reasoning machinery was operating in overdrive. I could not stop "looking" at that miracle of a thing, trying to somehow articulate its implications in language. But it was impossible. I thought to myself: "this is not meant for human consumption." The mere attempt at articulating it was exhaustive. I noticed I was – and I cannot avoid the expression – frying my brain to a crisp. It was overwhelming and painful in a non-physical way. I thought I would go insane, and it dawned on me that this is what insanity may feel like. Yet, I felt as though my mysterious alter ego were aware of how dangerous and distressing this kind of knowledge could be, and were somehow controlling the "dose," if you will. That was a reassuring thought, whether factual or not.

I concluded with certainty then that one must be literally insane in order to comprehend this thing. The magnitude of it, its hyper-dimensional character, and its implications, cannot be apprehended unless one completely abandons all pre-existing mental models, semantic frameworks, assumptions, and paradigms of thought one holds. Losing all this mental infrastructure comes very close to the definition of mental pathology. In fact, I understood then why ego dissolution appeared to be a necessary pre-requisite for exposure to that miraculous pattern: the preconceptions, expectations, and closed thought paradigms of the ego would prevent one from even seeing the pattern for what it is, let alone understanding it. The ego would dress it up and squeeze it into lower-dimensional models that would limit the perception of its true nature. Perhaps the mandalas I saw in inner theater were but such lower-dimensional, fragmentary projections or resonances of that miraculous pattern. Perhaps the mandala drawings used by mystics the world over are even lower-dimensional projections of it. There seems to be a hierarchical progression of states of consciousness leading to the state that made such understanding possible: from consensus reality, to the inner theater of mind, to ego dissolution, to this.

At some point, I could no longer bear to "understand" any more. I actively tried to abort the experience. Usually, holding on to the non-ordinary state of consciousness is delicate, so exiting it is straight-forward. But this time I was so deep in it that it took me some resolve. As in my first experiment, the return was somewhat disorienting. Yet, since I had been through it all before, I now recognized the process and told myself that I just had to hold on tight for a little while and I would soon feel better.

Now, as I write these words, I face the formidable challenge to try and articulate the unfathomable. Whatever I do, I am certain that more than 99% of the meaning, nuances, and richness of what I perceived have been lost upon the precarious imprinting of the impressions onto my brain. But I will do my best. The following paragraphs represent my feeble attempt at articulating some of what was instantaneously obvious to me merely upon "glancing" at the indescribable pattern I referred to earlier. The words capture but a very modest part of the pattern's self-evident and far-reaching implications. I do not know *how* an abstract pattern could entail or imply so much concrete information. I will simply record this information here as I recall it, with suspended judgment and critique about its validity. Later we will have occasion for rational analysis.

All of existence seems to emanate from a single Source in a radially symmetric manner. The elusive Source corresponds metaphorically to the center of a self-generating mandala. The diversity of existence somehow seems to correspond to the recursive unfolding of the Source according to a precise law defined by the geometric order encoded in it. Each aspect of existence, we included, may be but saliencies of this unfolding cosmic pattern, occupying different orbits in its radially-symmetric structure. Some aspects of existence orbit closer to the Source, others further away. But all are emanations of It.

There seems to be a trick to reality. Reality may be like a stage play: it is not quite what it purports to be; it seems autonomous and self-contained unless you change your perspective and look at the spectacle from backstage. Then you realize that the play is just the visible part – the façade, if you will – of an ingenious production, itself far more complex than the part that can be ordinarily experienced. Suddenly, you reassess the entire play under a new light. You understand what it was all about and how it came to being. You understand the process that led to its realization. This is a perspective that unifies and clarifies every-thing you thought of as multiple and diverse mysteries before. The trick behind our reality seems to lie somehow in the geometric formation principle governing the unfolding of the Source; such principle being encoded in a hyper-dimensional, abstract pattern. The variety of existence seems to be reducible to that one principle.[2]

All of reality seems to be the unfolding of a thought pattern in the imagination. Thought patterns seem to be the vehicle for the unfolding of the Source and the raw material of nature. Non-ordinary states of consciousness may be analogous to incom-mensurably powerful microscopes: they allow us to "magnify" reality to the point where an underlying realm of elemental thoughts becomes directly cognizable. Unlike atoms, these primary, universal building blocks of manifestation are minded, in the sense that the "stuff" they are made of is "mind stuff." As such, they are compliant to conscious *intent* like little soldiers of a highly disciplined toy army. These elemental thought patterns are like figments of the imagination of the Source. It is as though the Source thought in a language of abstract patterns and Its thoughts were one with reality. Therefore, reality may be the dream of the Source. We may be part of, and live in, that dream. Our consciousness and imagination, as salient segments of the unraveling consciousness and imagination of the Source, seem to be both subject and object of this process.

There seems to be no distinction between the process of

perceiving and the process of conceiving. Only what can be conceived and articulated, even if only implicitly, can be perceived. The entire unfolding of the Source seems to be a process of concurrent conception and perception. Its creation is a perception mirror of the Source's conception potential. Therefore, the idea of strong objectivity may be an illusion of our realm of reality. In other words, the idea that one can first perceive impartially, and only thereafter attempt to articulate and explain what has been perceived, appears to be fallacious. The perception of a phenomenon may necessarily entail an ability to articulate or explain that phenomenon at some level, implicitly or tentatively as it may be. That which cannot be articulated in some way cannot be perceived and, therefore, does not have reality. As such, perception is a mirror of our own cognitive machinery and conceptual dictionary. The broader is our dictionary of concepts and our ability to articulate these concepts according to a model or story, the more we can actually perceive. This, however, entails an inherent risk in our efforts to explain reality: the more we rely on certain models or stories, the more our perceptions will confirm those very models and stories, for our perceptions mirror them. This way, cognition may be, to some extent, a self-fulfilling and self-reinforcing process. Moreover, if we expect any new discoveries to remain consistent with our current models of reality, then, by construction, these new discoveries may be such that this expectation will be fulfilled at some level. Those with the most open minds, and a sincere *expectation* – more than a mere wish – to find something truly disconcerting, stand the best chance of making the most groundbreaking and confounding discoveries. Communication seems to play a crucial role in this context: it is an entropic force that will tend to minimize the heterogeneity of cognitive models and expectations. In other words, the more communication there is between conscious entities, the more their models and expectations about the nature and possibilities of reality will be synchronized and homogenized. Consequently, their perceptions of reality will also be harmonized with one another, creating the very consistency of reporting that seems to substantiate the notion of objectivity. In a society where communication is nearly instantaneous and widespread, it would be reasonable to expect that such homogenization of cognitive models would be nearly complete, therefore strongly – yet falsely – supporting the idea that objectivity is true. In this context, unexplained phenomena and other anomalies, when authentic, may be either the fragile perceptual feedback we get when our collective cognitive machinery has made a small step towards broadening its ability to conceive, or the reminiscent differences in the cognitive models of different members of a society. The implications of all this are profound.

The patterns that underlie reality seem to be fractal.[3] This seems to reflect the ancient saying that, "as above, so below." After all, fractals are self-similar patterns: a segment of a fractal looks like the whole fractal, albeit at a different level (see Figure 5). Each one of us may be a segment of the universal, unfolding, fractal mandala; a segment self-similar to the whole but at a lower level; a segment we can perceive symbolically as our own inner theater when in a non-ordinary state of consciousness. The mandalas of my inner theater were, I suspect, a symbolic representation of the segment of this cosmic fractal that corresponds to me as an entity. Since perception and cognition seem to be equivalent, each one of us may also project onto our respective inner theater whatever it is that we can conceive it to be. In my case, I have projected planetary systems and proto-conscious Christmas balls in a domed inner chamber.

The impressions I have collected during this experiment have

Figure 5. A computer-generated fractal. Notice that parts of the fractal are smaller copies of the whole fractal.

been confounding. The foundations of my own worldview, of my model of reality, have wobbled and cracked under their sheer weight. Right now, I do not know where the implications of these new impressions will take me. But they could be – and I do not take this statement lightly – life-changing.

Chapter 9

Fourth experiment: Bathing in that we are made of

I came into this experience with a very open mind, clear of expectations about what I should accomplish. This stemmed from the fact that, having had such a transcendent experience in my previous attempt, I did not know what else to seek. So I let my mind free to drift as the transition into a non-ordinary state of consciousness began. So relaxed was I this time that I immediately slid into hypnagogia. Upon noticing this and trying to retain my lucidity, the suspicion immediately arose in my mind that I probably visit my inner theater during regular sleep cycles. Perhaps the familiarity I felt with that place was not only due to old memories, but due to recent ones as well. *Perhaps all my dreams were projections onto the screen of inner theater*. Perhaps I just could not remember, in the morning, where I had been or how I had gotten there. Regular dreams, like the experiences of other non-ordinary states of consciousness, are very fleeting and elusive in that we tend to forget them very quickly.

The difference between regular dreams and the experience I was now undergoing was the following: in regular dreams, we seem to lose the capacity to reason according to the standard constraints of consensus reality – namely, the laws of logic and physics. During a lucid experience of a non-ordinary state of consciousness, on the other hand, we largely retain those abilities. Other than this difference, both states can be surprisingly similar phenomenologically. A lucid, non-ordinary state of consciousness can be just as free-minded as a regular dream. Both are also difficult to remember and articulate afterwards. Both come accompanied by the feeling of belonging to a different reality, not quite like what we experience during ordinary waking states, but nonetheless no less real.

After this observation, it became more difficult to hold on to lucidity and I slid further into an experience that seemed to last days, though that was obviously not the case in objective reality. I felt as if I had drifted in time and space, experiencing what felt like different moments in history, and feeling as if I were different people. I could not recognize these other people nor see their faces; the experience was more subtle. I simply recall having that ineffable feeling of the inner life of another person: the feeling of a different body shape, of different ideas, world-views and paradigms of thought, of different emotions and motivations, different psychological scars, etc. I seemed to have little control of this process and, for a moment, I entirely forgot the context of consensus reality where I was located, becoming fully immersed in the experience just like in a regular dream. Sometimes I felt as if I were in different countries; other times in very different and truly bizarre places that I could not recognize nor describe in words.

The mandalas and spinning Kandinsky scintillae that occupied my inner theater during previous experiences now seemed to take coherent form, clumping together and self-trans-forming to compose fantastically beautiful spacescapes in a kind of cosmic morphogenesis (see Figure 6). Images of alien, unrec-ognized landscapes and cities would then coalesce from within those: magnificent skylines of smooth, high-rising architecture coated with an iridescent, aura-like fog irradiating the colors of the rainbow; an iridescent fog contrasted against the dark skies of a non-refractive atmosphere bathed in sunshine (see Figure 7). Planets, stars, and nebulae could be seen in the background. Many of these amazingly beautiful images followed one another, melting and morphing into one another in fluidic motion. Some could easily be, or so it felt to me, real landscapes of distant places. Others were more akin to the output of an

Figure 6. Computer art resembling images of cosmic morpho-genesis.

Figure 7. Computer art resembling images of alien landscapes.

extraordinarily creative, artistic mind not my own, which I was having the privilege to observe. Was there even a difference between these two possibilities? I knew not.

Recovering some lucidity, the thought occurred to me that consciousness was surely a non-local phenomenon in both time and space. That is, I had the certainty that consciousness was not limited to the here and now of my physical brain but could, under certain circumstances, gain awareness of places and times beyond, whether real or imaginary – the difference between real and imaginary, once again, appearing nonsensical to me.

I wondered then if I could steer this drift in time and space. Could I bring myself, through intentional visualization, to "remember" my distant past or "return" to places I had not been to in a long time? I formed the intent to return to a particular moment of my childhood. Another self-transformation of the images ensued, as if they were made of a highly malleable and compliant material, and a different point of space-time crystal-lized before me. I was back at the brackish water lagoon where I used to go fishing when I was a kid. Those were some of my fondest memories; periods of absolute simplicity, peace, contentment, and total communion with nature. I could again hear the delicate sounds of the water ripples splashing against the rocks where I used to set myself up. I could feel the gentle breeze against my face, the sound of the fresh air flowing gently round my earlobes. How peaceful. For all cognitive purposes, I was there again.

I continued this exercise for what felt like a long time, willfully returning to various places, moments, people, and circumstances of my past that were of particular significance to me. Inevitably, eventually the memory of one of the most intense experiences of my life began rising in my awareness: that of falling in love with the person who today is my wife. This time, however, the experience was entirely one of inner feeling, not of physical perception. I was just overtaken by the inner warmth and the sense of wholeness that seem to characterize the act of falling in love with someone. And then the experiment took me to the next level; one that, at that moment, I was not expecting. Somehow, the feeling of falling in love with a particular person keyed my consciousness into what I can only describe as a kind of universal "tone," or specific vibration. By remembering the feeling of falling in love, I latched onto that apparently external vibration of pure subjective feeling. It then amplified what I was feeling in a kind of sympathetic resonance. My own feelings and this "tone" seemed to be reinforcing one another in a positive feedback loop. Though I do not like to use the word "love," because it is so overloaded with loose semantics and charged with shallow and cheap sentimentalism, I am unable to find any other suitable word. Indeed, and I blush to say this, I felt as though I was falling in love with the entire universe. There was, of course, nothing sexual about it; just a feeling of profound belonging and integration. It was as though the entire universe were one incommensurable, connected, living structure, and I somehow were a part of it like a cell is a part of my body.

The sensation of a vibration was still there. It seemed not only to accompany the experience but to be the source of it somehow. It was as though I had tapped into the backbone of the universal manifold of vibrating subjectivity. I could feel this "tone" as a gentle but nonetheless strong, full, irresistible hum resonating everywhere. It felt wonderfully pleasurable. It seemed to provide everything needed to sustain one's existence.

I might have forgotten to say that I underwent this experience while reclined in an adjustable bed, alone in a very dark and very quiet room. In that comfortable position, I felt absolute contentment with the feeling of this vibratory "tone" running through my body and mind. Frankly, at that moment, I would not have exchanged that feeling for anything in this world of ours. It was sufficient in all ways that "sufficient" can be interpreted. And it felt like a recognizable dream that I thought I probably had before. This was not the first time I was having this wonderful feeling. I had just forgotten it. Yet, I was in full possession of my reasoning skills at that moment. I knew exactly who I was, what I was doing, and how I had gotten there. I could think about the experience as lucidly and logically as I can think about it now. And I found it marvelous, confounding, beyond the explanatory power of my models of reality.

This experiment was unique in many ways, but one in particular seems more significant: unlike my previous attempts, which all seemed to transport me to a different, ineffable, perhaps hyper-dimensional realm of subjective reality, this experience was pretty much grounded in our familiar three dimensions of space and one dimension of time. Though extra-ordinary in many ways, particularly as far as its apparent non-locality and its profound emotional content, it never departed from the framework, references, and archetypes of regular life and standard space-time.

As that wonderful vibration was running through me, resonating with me, I felt as if I were being charged up like a battery connected to the electricity mains. This feeling of being charged could no less validly be described as a feeling of being fed, consoled, loved, or healed. All these things seemed to be equivalent. At the same time, the strange idea popped into my mind that perhaps I was made of the very substance of this "tone." Perhaps all things we see and feel, even we ourselves, are like vibratory ripples in an ocean of a single substance. Perhaps this tone was the natural frequency of vibration – the funda-mental note – of this ocean, whose oscillation sustains, through sympathetic resonance, all harmonic notes around it, whatever their octaves. Perhaps this is why I had the subjective impression that all things in the universe were somehow connected. Perhaps all we need to do to heal ourselves, I thought, is to tune in to this fundamental note and simply let it do what it does. A phrase popped in my head, fully formed: "All we need to do to heal ourselves is to bathe in that we are made of." All we need to do is to stop trying and, instead, allow ourselves to enter into resonance with this fundamental note of existence. The overarching theme of this thought: healing does not require action, effort, or trying, much to the contrary. It seemed to be an entirely passive process, there lying the main difficulty in achieving it. I sensed a fractal order of vibratory hierarchies in which the same principles applied self-similarly at all levels of the hierarchy. The planet could also heal itself by bathing in that it is made of, it seemed to me. I cannot point out exactly where I got this idea from.

I could have remained in that state of bliss forever if biological necessities had not taken me out of it. Returning to regular consciousness was not difficult this time: the entire experience had taken place within the context of regular space-time anyway. Once back, I quickly began feeling a strong longing for that state of attunement to the main universal artery of contentment and warmth. But all that was left was the need to adjust to the reality that such occasions are special and ephemeral.

Chapter 10

Stepping back and pondering

As I begin to write this chapter, it has been a few months since I last attempted an experiment with non-ordinary states of consciousness. The idea has been to take a step back and then try and make sense of the experiences from a rational, balanced perspective. The underlying premise is that the extra perspective allowed by the passage of time will have improved my judgment and interpretation of the results.

Yet I struggle with such premise. It appears to me that I had a broader capacity of thought and perception while in non-ordinary states of consciousness than I have now. So should I trust the conclusions I arrive at now over the conclusions I arrived at during or immediately after the experiments themselves? Should I trust the perspective gained with time over the earlier, fresher, uncontaminated recollections and insights acquired from direct experience? This seems to be a question inherent to subjective exploration and I sincerely do not know the correct answer for it. What I do know is that there are growing shifts in my ontological inclinations as the experiments slip further into the past. Nonetheless, let us try to distil the key elements that seem to consistently run through the subjective data at hand, as discussed in the four previous chapters. The lines below are my attempt to strike a balance and integrate the ideas I had immediately following each experiment with those evolved long thereafter, while trying to remain honest to both perspectives.

The reader should also bear in mind that, in the spirit of subjective exploration, the lines below merely reflect a very personal thought process whose conclusions can be valid for me, as the experiencer of the subjective data at hand, but perhaps for nobody else. *Subjective exploration entails no general theses or claims of objective truth.* My sharing of the thoughts below is simply an attempt to illustrate – for what it is worth – a personal struggle to resolve and integrate very personal experiences. I am not trying to convince anyone of anything, nor am I attempting to defend the validity of my conclusions for others.

Okay, let us now get on with it. I believe my experiences could be classified into four different levels, or "realms," depending on how far removed from consensus reality their gestalts were. The one closest to our regular perceptions was that of the fourth experiment. In it, though I had extraordinary feelings of connectedness, visions of alien worlds, and memories of lives not my own, the experiences were composed of familiar 3D visual elements and emotional archetypes. The notion of linear time was also preserved. As an extraordinarily realistic dream, the experience was at the same time real and imaginary, without contradiction. I will thus call this level "dreamland," for lack of a better word.

The next level was what I called "inner theater" in my first and second experiments: a place that one's mind recognizes as the ground of its existence. It is perceived as the limit case of familiarity. In that place, the ego can survive, though one's perception of the self is usually enriched. The inner theater could be either a coherent state of mind – embodying the emotional and perceptual content intrinsically associated with being in it – or a coherent segment of the space-time continuum perceived *directly* through consciousness,[1] without mediation of the five senses. *One must wonder if there actually is a difference between these two alternatives.* In either case, there seems to be an undeniable, self-evident relationship between inner theater and the most primordial manifestation of one's being. While in it, one seems both to *inhabit* and to *be* one's own inner theater; an identity between object and subject that is impossible to artic-

93

ulate clearly in words, but which is felt in a very unambiguous way. Indeed, it is tempting to speculate that one's consciousness inhabits or emanates from one's inner theater, at the same time giving it its existence. It is also tempting to speculate, on the basis of the subjective data at hand, that the inner theater is not causally dependent on the physical body or brain; that it precedes the body both ontologically and in time, even if it is "merely" a state of mind. Naturally, that would imply that mind is not generated by the brain, but in some other way associated with brain processes while we experience ordinary states of consciousness. Such implication is indeed very consistent with the gestalt of each experiment. The experience of inner theater, while still relatively time-bound and allowing for the survival of the ego, seems to transcend the three dimensions of space we normally experience. I am unsure whether to think of it as an *extra*-dimensional experience entirely outside of space, or a *hyper*-dimensional experience taking place in a broader spatial framework. Since the latter is the only one still conducive – precariously as it may be – to the description of visual impressions, I am forced to adopt it throughout this book.

The next level, experienced at the end of my first experiment, transcends not only space but the notions of linear time and ego as well. Indeed, there seems to be at least two distinct forms of identity that consciousness can take on, both of which we recognize as the "I." The first, and the one usually experienced during ordinary states of consciousness, is the "I" of the ego; the "I" of the cognitive models constructed by the brain. The second is an "I" that seems to be independent of the ego and of life in linear time; a transcendent "I" that seems to exist entirely beyond time, space, and life itself, and whose identity is more profoundly recognized as the true "I" than the relatively provincial and flattened notions of the ego. The implication of this is that a hypothetical, universal field of consciousness must somehow "clot" into multiple, separate "focal points" in a realm of reality beyond that of the physical brain. Each of these focal points must then correspond to a transcendent "I" that is coupled, in awareness, to the electrochemical signals of an individual brain and its ego constructs.

The most transcendent level I have reached was that described in my third experiment: a level that seems to break through the hyper-dimensional boundaries of inner theater and allow one to peek into the underlying mechanisms of reality. These are then presented in the form of an indescribable, evolving *Pattern* (which, from now on, I will consistently write with a capital "P" to discriminate it from other uses of the word "pattern"). There lie the answers to all things real and imaginary. At that level – which cannot be reached while one is dressed in the clothes of the ego and carrying the mental baggage we normally associate to sanity – one is confronted with deep, unspeakable truths about what, why, and how things are what they are. This level transcends manifested reality in all its forms, objective or imaginary. It allows one to look at the backstage of the play and discover its secrets. Intellect cannot survive this confrontation for very long.

Having classified the experiences in four levels of transcendence, let us try and look for overarching themes that could help us structure and categorize the data at hand. The first theme seems to be that of paradoxes, the resolution of which entails the dissolution of polarities; the union of opposites in an intellectually contradictory but experientially unambiguous way. The least transcendent instance of this theme occurred in my fourth experiment, when the dichotomy between dream and reality, between conception and externalization, was blurred. This blurring was not an invalidation of either dream or reality. In other words, I am saying neither that nothing is real nor that dreams are perceptions of some realm of objective reality. No. What I am saying is: first, that dreams can perhaps take on increasing levels of properties normally associated with reality

– namely, concreteness, endurance, autonomy, etc.; *and* second, that reality can perhaps take on increasing levels of properties normally associated with dreams – namely, malleability, acquiescence to intent, etc. In other words, the subjective data suggests that dreams and reality may simply be different points on a single, continuous spectrum of the same underlying "stuff;" much like red and blue are simply different points on the electromagnetic spectrum of light.

There is another occurrence of this theme. While many of my experiences at the "dreamland" level were clearly past memories or constructed out of pictorial elements familiar to my ego, some seemed entirely foreign to me: coherent memories of other lives, images of other worlds, cognition models not my own, etc. This raises the possibility that such experiences, while indeed imaginary in nature, may also reflect conscious impressions tapped from the universal memory of qualia. The hypothesis is that the transcendent "I" can tap into this universal repository of transpersonal experiences just as easily as the ego can tap into personal memory. Upon doing so, the tapped memories are then projected onto the screen of mind just as the products of creative imagination. So the experiences one undergoes transcend the differences between transpersonal memory and creative imagination. In other words, it is hard to say whether what one is experiencing is the *creation* of a new story or the *replay*, or even reconstruction, of a transpersonal story remembered. My own intuition is that it is somehow *both*, concurrently and without contradiction, paradoxically as this may sound. Indeed, in a realm where reality is imagined, *memories* and *creations* differ only by their position in the linear arrow of time: memories are located in the past and creations in the future. But *both* are the products of the imagination. If one can move freely back and forth along the arrow of time, the difference between the two becomes thus meaningless: *in dreamland, there is only the unfolding of transpersonal imagination; past, present, and perhaps future.*

This same theme – that is, the resolution of paradoxes and dichotomies – can be seen yet again at the level of inner theater, where the experience is *both* perceived as an exteriorized reality *and* as the unfolding of the experienc*er*. When the object is in fact an unfolding of the subject, the subject's dreams become his or her experienced reality. While the "I" *inhabits* its own inner theater of mentality, such inner theater *is* itself the unfolding of the mentality of the "I" in a manner that completely transcends the duality of subject and object. Indeed, the reality of inner theater seems entirely acquiescent to the emotions and imagination of the "I:" what the latter feels and imagines is externalized by projection onto the fabric of that inner space, taking on the form of almost autonomous, enduring phenomena. This, it seems to me, is why my experiences, particularly in the first and second experiments, seemed so colored by my own expectations and interpretations.

The implication of the transcendence of object-subject duality in inner theater, and of the fact that what is experienced there seems to be a projection of pure mentality, is that the very *substance* of its reality is pure thought. And here is where the second overarching theme of these experiences comes into play. Indeed, *the subjective data at hand suggests that thought patterns are the underlying building blocks of everything experienced*. Let us explore this in a little more depth.

One of my strongest intuitions, after having undergone these experiments, is that *the mandalas and other geometric forms experienced in inner theater are visual cognitions of raw, elemental thought patterns*.[2] In my first two experiments, though the emotional content of the experience was very concrete and recognizable, the visual impressions were entirely abstract. If the inner theater is made of thought, then these geometrically represented, elemental thought patterns are the building blocks underlying its reality. The information comprised in these raw thought patterns is represented by the internal relationships intrinsic to their geometric characteristics, like the proportions, relative positions, angles, and intersections of its constituent parts. Such geometric relationships are the purest expression of thought, independent of context and unaltered by culture or education. They are entirely self-contained representations of manifested information, requiring no external semantic grounding. As such, they break the circular deadlock science is forever confined to: *elemental thought patterns do not need to be explained in terms of anything else; they are self-contained embodiments of their own meaning.* They are what is left at the end of reduction; the knife that slices through the Ouroboros' tail.[3] How this can be so is something that cannot be satisfactorily explained, but only experienced firsthand. Through abstract geometry, our basic library of elemental thought patterns takes on an "externalized," concrete, perceivable reality in the environment of inner theater.

While I perceived these elemental thought patterns in and by themselves at the level of "inner theater," at the less transcendent level of "dreamland" – as in my fourth experiment – they seemed to have *coalesced* to form coherent, concrete images in the screen of mind; images I cognized as those not only of my distant past, but also of alien worlds and unrecognized lives. It seems thus that *elemental thought patterns are the building blocks of the compositions of the imagination on the screen of mind.* They are, if you will, akin to the elements in a "periodic table of thought" which, in turn, can be used to compose imagined realities. Once a coherent composition is imagined, the underlying elemental thought patterns disappear. They become as much an abstraction as the atoms of oxygen and hydrogen felt when one runs one's fingers through water: all that is then left to perception is the freshness, texture, and fluidity of the water, not the abstract idea of microscopic systems of neutrons, protons, and orbiting electrons. Similarly, the geometric forms of the elemental thought patterns seem to disappear from the compositions of the imagination once these compositions are formed. In this context, perhaps the mad, spinning "Kandinsky scintillae" of inner theater, with their seemingly absurd behavior, were simply unguided and chaotic interactions of elemental thought patterns before they coalesced and self-organized into the coherent, imagined realities of "dreamland." This also seems to satisfactorily explain the character of senselessness and silliness associated with these geometric artifacts during my second experiment: the incoherent interactions of elemental thought patterns are indeed senseless and silly unless and until organized by purposeful intent into meaningful stories.

It seems to me that the causal agency of the coalescence of elemental thought patterns into coherent images and storylines is *intention*. The application of intention entails focus. By intending we bring focus, direction, and coherence to a continuous process of creation in the imagination, whose dynamics may persist whether it is coordinated or not. By intending we cause the elemental thought patterns to align, self-organize, and fall into order. By intending we take the steering wheel of their behavior and give it coherent form. When not intending, their dynamics may continue but without direction or coherence. The creative process of the imagination may be non-stoppable; it may be its very nature to continuously unfold. Perhaps our only option is intentional visualization: to bring our own imagination into focus and give it direction.

The remarkable implication of all this is that, in inner theater, one can visually cognize the raw materials of thought: the pure, unaltered, basic thought forms out of which the images of inner space coalesce. Mandalas, with their characteristic radial symmetries, seem to be the strongest visual representation of these mental building blocks. They are the basic vocabulary, or the basic set of archetypes, of the imagination. The "essays" made out of this basic vocabulary are the direct result of the application of intention to the composition of mental stories. To use a mathematical metaphor from the field of linear algebra, the information contained in the elemental thought patterns may be the orthonormal basis that spans the entire space of one's imagination. That such ultimate abstraction can take concrete, observable form suggests that *all thoughts, no matter how abstract, are intrinsically manifestable and perceivable as "externalized" realities.*

The subjective data also suggests that the elemental thought patterns seen in inner theater are but fractal segments, or resonances, of the underlying Pattern unfolding from the Source. This way, one's inner theater may be but a local segment of the fractal whole, whereof all segments are, in a way, an image of the whole itself. As above, so below. The mandala patterns of inner theater may be lower-dimensional, flattened projections, like shadows, of salient segments of the underlying Pattern. This may be the mechanism of the apparent unity of all things. Indeed, the subjective perception of mandalas in inner theater and of the unfolding Pattern were qualitatively similar, except in that the latter seemed to have a much higher-dimensional and broader character. If the patterns of inner theater span the space of one's personal imagination, the Pattern unfolding from the Source must span the space of all existence. It may reflect the thought language of the Unified Mind whose imagination shapes all existence.

On the basis of these very personal speculations, *I believe the four levels of transcendence discussed earlier – namely, "dreamland," "inner theater," "transcendent I," and the "Source" – correspond to a scale of increasing deconstruction of phenomena into their underlying, abstract building blocks of thought.* In "dreamland," all perceptions are compound, coalesced structures projected onto a (mental) low-dimensional space-time fabric. In "inner theater," the underlying elemental thought patterns behind these coalesced structures become perceivable in and by themselves, in their natural, higher-dimensional state. The "transcendent I" sheds the flat cognition models of the ego – which are based on coalesced concepts – enabling one to cognize the next level. Finally, at the level of the "Source," one can glimpse at the fractal whole of which all elemental thought patterns are mere saliencies, resonances, or partial projections. This way, the technologies of awareness expansion may indeed be analogous to microscopes and telescopes in the sense that they allow one to see – with some noise and difficulty in clearly registering and interpreting these images – beyond the coarse appearances of coalesced thought structures. They may allow one to see not only the very small or the very big, but beyond small and big, towards the extra dimensions of what is behind these appearances.

The scale of deconstruction discussed above provides an integrated hierarchy of reduction. Traversing this hierarchy along the direction of increasing coalescence of thought patterns, one can build a perceptual world much akin to consensus reality, except in that it embodies the malleability of dreams. Traversing this hierarchy along the opposite direction leads to pure, abstract, self-contained, unified thought. The rules of coalescence across the hierarchy seem amenable to geometric representation. Such a feeble, tentative, and precarious model for reducing dreams to geometric abstractions is my best attempt, as of the time I wrote these words, at resolving and integrating my experiences into a coherent framework.

Before moving on, however, we must return to a question raised earlier. While it is difficult to objectively demonstrate the ontological validity of a subjective experience, one can ask whether an influx of knowledge has taken place that cannot be explained by brain-hosted memories or sensory stimuli. It is my strong inclination, on the basis of the subjective data at hand, that indeed knowledge and impressions previously not present in my brain have been accessed through non-ordinary states of consciousness. These images and understandings so far transcend everything entailed by consensus reality that I cannot imagine they were generated by my brain. That said, the question of objectively proving that such impressions were real, in the naïve way we normally understand reality to be, is a different matter. To do that would require confirmation *in consensus reality* of impressions acquired in non-ordinary states of consciousness. For instance, upon seeing the image of a foreign place during subjective exploration, one could try and find that place in the physical world to confirm that the images originally perceived do correspond to a real place. Then – and only if it could be verified that one had never been to that place before, nor seen any pictures of it – the reality of the impression received could be objectively demonstrated. However, the impressions one receives during subjective exploration tend to significantly transcend consensus reality and, therefore, cannot be confirmed in consensus reality. Even the impressions of "dreamland" described in the fourth experiment report, which seemed mostly grounded in the framework of 3D space and linear time, were either impossible to pin down to a specific location and timeframe or very alien in nature. Therefore, there is to be no closure here: I cannot firmly and objectively conclude that there was an influx of *real* and *external* impressions into my brain during the experiments. What remains is the strong intuition that that was indeed the case.

Another point worth emphasizing here is the fact that most of the experiences reported were subjectively registered as *remembrances*, as opposed to *discoveries*. That was completely unexpected and caught me off guard. Several times, because there seemed to be nothing really surprising going on during an experiment, I would conclude it had been a failure; just to realize, to my own astonishment, upon returning to consensus reality, how bizarre the whole thing had been. Even the notion of a transcendent "I" beyond time and space, which I would normally think of as an abstract "other person" foreign to me, has been felt as an unambiguous *remembrance* of who I *really* am and have been all along. I find this fascinating and perhaps the most important and unique characteristic of subjective exploration that sets it apart from science. Allow me to try and explain why.

As a former professional scientist, I used not to take other people's claims of transcendent experiences very seriously. Despite my hidden curiosity, I could always think of a thousand ways to dismiss, trivialize, or explain the whole thing away. Looking back at it now, I think what enabled this attitude was the implicit assumption that what one experiences in those cases is separate from one's self and therefore amenable to objective analysis. I could not understand why those people would insist on taking their experiences at face value. Why would they not critically assess the suspiciousness of the whole thing? That seemed unreasonable and, frankly, plain irrational to me.

However, when one experiences a new insight as an unambiguous, long-term memory of a self-evident truth, one is entirely disarmed. The shield of objective rationality melts effortlessly like butter under the sun. Yes, the experience is unexplained and therefore highly suspicious, but it served merely to *trigger a memory* that was already an integral part of one's being. Or so it seems. This swiftly makes the whole thing very personal. Suddenly, it does not matter anymore whether the experience is suspicious or not, *for one can now remember the essence of the insight as an independent memory that far preceded the experience itself.* Invalidating the circumstances of the experience is, logically, not sufficient to invalidate a memory that precedes the experience. One's own memory, when recovered in such an unambiguous manner, ought to be taken seriously and render all other questions secondary, valid as those questions may be. It becomes impossible to take distance. It becomes impossible to extricate the experience away from oneself in order to analyze it coldly and objectively. Hypothetical scenarios sought to invalidate or trivialize the insight received are no longer mere abstractions of cold rationality, but contradict one's own felt memories; one's remembered convictions. It is no longer easy to take these hypothetical scenarios seriously.

This is what makes a direct, first-person, transcendent experience impossible to ignore or rationalize away. This is what makes it stick even when one cannot come up with an explanation for it nor defend its reliability. All these questions become secondary the moment one identifies the insight with what one has, deep inside, somehow *known all along*. What else might we have always known? *Who might we find in the mirror when we remember it all*? It is personal, very personal indeed.

Chapter 11

Imagining the reality of dreams

Even though it is admittedly a projection of the psyche, the experience of dreamland is remarkably palpable, playing itself out autonomously to one's perfectly lucid observation. That a projection of the psyche can be thus unequivocally perceived as an externalized, objective reality is thought provoking. As a matter of fact, this is a notion we all share: regular dreams can be equally indistinguishable from ordinary reality. Imagine, therefore, that there is no fundamental difference between the realms of dreamland and inner theater on the one hand, and our consensus reality on the other hand. This would imply that dreamland and inner theater are actual segments of the same space-time continuum we live in. Perhaps the space-time continuum has other, hidden dimensions not accessible to our five senses. Perhaps the only way to gain awareness of those hyper-dimensional segments of the continuum is through the *direct* awareness gained with non-ordinary states of consciousness. What might we then infer from it?

If those transcendent realms are indeed part of the *same* space-time *continuum* of consensus reality, then there is no reason to believe that the underlying reality of those realms is any different from the underlying reality of our supposedly objective world. Therefore, it would be an intriguing exercise to extrapolate whatever one learns about those transcendent realms to the realm of our consensus reality. Based on our discussion thus far, that would entail that consensus reality is, just like the reality of dreamland and inner theater, *also* the result of our imaginations at work.

I am perfectly aware of how unlikely a possibility this seems to be. It seems to contradict observation and it certainly flies in the face of our cultural assumptions and models. So why would anyone even consider an outrageous idea like that? For two reasons: First, and most importantly, because upon one's return from non-ordinary states of consciousness such idea does not seem outrageous at all. Once the distortive and myopic glasses of culture and convention are removed, one's own mind accepts the possibility of such idea without fuzz. Second, and perhaps more circumstantially, because science itself has been confronted with the fact that repeated experimental results seem to contradict the premise that reality is independent of our minds. For instance, strong theoretical and experimental evidence against the notion of an objective reality has been presented, surprisingly matter-of-factly, by a team of Austrian and Polish physicists in 2007. Their analysis and results have been published in the most renowned of peer-reviewed scientific journals, *Nature*.[1] One cannot help but wonder why extraordinary results like this do not cause a popular media stir and force our civilization to at least question its reigning worldviews.

It is indeed striking how one's thoughts and feelings seem to take on a life of their own in the realm of dreamland. They become externalized in the sense that one can observe them just as a spectator observes a theatrical play; not very different from the way we experience consensus reality. In dreamland, thoughts acquire a kind of autonomy, or "inertia," in the sense that their storylines persist and unfold on the screen of mind even when one initially tries to think about something else. Moreover, unlike regular dreams, one witnesses this externalization of the imagination in full, lucid, reasoning awareness. What makes it all so extraordinary is that, while one is witnessing fantastic worlds unfold before one's eyes, *one knows that it is all a projection of the psyche*. Now that gives you pause for thought: *How far does the power of the psyche really go as far as projecting a seemingly externalized reality around us?* Once one has had an experience like that of dreamland, which blurs the boundaries between the properties we normally attribute to reality and those we attribute to dreams, one softens to the possibility that maybe reality is indeed a kind of persisting dream; one simply with a yet higher degree of "inertia" than the stories of dreamland. Instead of being opposites, dreams and reality are perceived to be different points in a *continuous spectrum* of degrees of externalization and the kind of "inertia" discussed above.

Even more confounding to our standard worldviews is the knowledge input one receives in inner theater and at the level of the "Source." There is an unambiguous realization, during the experience, that the impressions received in those realms apply to reality; *all reality.* One believes strongly that one has peeked at the secret of all existence; at something that explains our condition as a subset of a much broader reality. Indeed, the ineffable feeling one has upon returning from subjective exploration is that consensus reality is by far not the whole story; that we are not ordinarily aware of this fact simply because, while in the trance-like state of ordinary consciousness, we temporarily *forget* what the real deal is.

The way one arrives at conclusions while in non-ordinary states of consciousness seems more *direct* and, therefore, more reliable than our ordinary, rational thought processes. The former appears to come as a form of unmediated knowledge, while the latter is mediated by sensory input and modeling. Let me try to elucidate this idea a little more: In ordinary states of consciousness, all we are aware of is the processing of information – represented by electrochemical signals – taking place in our brains. We have no direct awareness of the external world, but only of the information about it that is captured by our five senses; you can verify the veracity of this statement simply by closing your eyes. After making observations, we iterate upon cognition models hosted by our brains until we converge to one that fits well with the observed information. It is then that we *infer* something about reality, believing to have understood it.[2] For instance, if one digs out a tree and observes a root system for the first time, one iterates upon different mental models until converging to a model that seems to explain a truth about trees: namely, that roots anchor a tree to the ground and keep it upright. This is a conclusion mediated by information (the sight of the root system dug out) and modeling (the synaptic connections that associate the sight of the roots to the idea of the tree standing upright). On the other hand, while in a non-ordinary state of consciousness, such mediation seems superfluous. One seems to gain *direct* awareness of certain facts. To use a somewhat precarious metaphor, it is as if one gained knowledge of the fact that roots keep trees standing upright without the need to ever see a root system or infer its function through synaptic associations. *One becomes directly aware of the conclusion, without need for any intermediary awareness of the precursors or correlates of such conclusion.* The potential pitfalls of inference are avoided. There are no intermediaries potentially polluting the purity of the original truth. Indeed, it is only *after* the non-ordinary conscious impression has been registered in awareness that one begins to *interpret* it by trying to match it against different mental models; that is, against different made-up stories about how nature must be put together.

Allow me to make an observation at this point. The value systems we developed and adopted in Western civilization are such that, contrary to what I argued above, *direct* understanding is actually considered highly suspicious and unreliable. That seems crazy: How can a more direct and less convoluted path to a conclusion be less reliable? *The problem arises when one seeks to convince others that his or her own revelations are the objective truth.* In other words, the problem is the attempt at *transferring* one's direct conclusions to others. After all, one's own direct insights are only meaningful to oneself; they are not transferable; they mean nothing to people who have not had the experience, and rightfully so. Therefore, *when it comes to establishing a common framework for the constructive co-existence of different individuals within a society, such things as rules of evidence are necessary.* In that context, direct understanding alone, without evidence, is not enough. This, in fact, was the key accomplishment of the European Enlightenment in the eighteenth century: it demanded *substantiation* from anyone bent on promoting his worldview as a truth that applied to others as well; it demanded more than the mere pronouncement of a revelation, but *evidence* with significance for people who had not had the revelation themselves. This was, and remains, crucial for the protection of individual liberties. It ensured, and continues to ensure, that society provides a suitable milieu for the pursuit of whatever purpose our individual lives may have in the greater scheme of things. Unfortunately, we, as individuals, allowed ourselves to extrapolate this useful social notion way too far: *we now dismiss the validity of our own, heartfelt, direct intuitions even when it comes to our own private worldviews.* That is a tragedy. A society that protects individual freedom is only as healthy as our use of that freedom; our willingness to live our own experiences and evolve our personal worldviews. After all, *all we have are our own insights and convictions.* Everything else is mere abstraction. Dismissing our personal insights and convictions amounts to the annihilation of ourselves in favor of an abstract – and ultimately unreal – statistical truth. It defeats whatever meaning our existence may have and is a recipe for psychological imbalance and distress. *A sane society that values individual freedom can only remain sane as long as its citizens value their own respective individualities and idiosyncratic experiences as well.* Finding this tricky balance between the rules of evidence that safeguard a sane society, and the acknowledgement of personal, direct insight that nurtures sane individuals, is a key challenge of our times.

Having digressed long enough, let us go back to the subject. What I am trying to say is the following: the gestalt of the experiences of subjective exploration entails that what one cognizes in a non-ordinary state of consciousness, through an influx of knowledge unmediated by sensory input and modeling, is the purest and most direct form of reality; our regular perceptions being a kind of stupor or daze. Even though this frame of mind does not seem to survive longer than a few days after each experiment, it inevitably makes one's mind more open to the outrageous possibility that we are all living, all the time, in a world of mind.

I am *not* outright submitting to you that the world is imaginary. This is *not* a book with a thesis; that is for science. All I am doing is inviting you to imagine extreme but well grounded *possibilities*, for the sake of intellectual enjoyment and the cultivation of creativity. Only *your own direct experiences* with subjective exploration can take *you* beyond speculation and towards *knowledge*. This book is no substitute for that. Instead, what I sought to achieve with it is a kind of art whose medium is *ideas*; an art form that, although expressed in words like a work of fiction, engages in intense flirtation with the here and now; so intense in fact that, as in an obsessive love affair, it seeks to dissolve the boundaries between itself and the object of its affection. Such an art form thrives in the possibility that it is one with reality.

In that spirit, let us further imagine that the unfolding of the Source generates our shared, consensus reality just as it does the reality of inner theater. What then?

Then ours is a reality of thought, built with the building blocks of elemental thought patterns and obeying the relationships embedded in their intrinsic geometry. Indeed, as I would find out in my research after the completion of my experiments, the idea that the world is a work of geometry is very old, having been developed in the ancient philosophy of Sacred Geometry.[3] It goes back in time perhaps as far as Plato. According to the creation myth of Sacred Geometry, Creation is a geometric pattern unfolding symmetrically from a dimensionless cosmic center, inherently mysterious and unknowable, identified with the Creator. While I do not recognize in my own experiences most of the particular elements entailed by Sacred Geometry, clear and intriguing echoes of such creation myth are obvious in my third experiment report. As Plato wrote in "Republic" (592), "there is laid up in heaven a pattern of the city within, which those who desire may behold."

The intuition that nature is constructed according to the symmetries of a pattern is pervasive even in science and has enabled important scientific discoveries. Indeed, as eloquently told by Professor Ian Stewart, the pursuit of modern science has, to a large extent, been the pursuit of abstract, mathematical symmetries.[4] Major discoveries have been made simply by following the tracks of "missing symmetries," even though there is no reason, in principle, why nature should follow those kinds of patterns. In an extreme example of this innate intuition, physicist Garrett Lisi has proposed a "theory of everything" predicting the existence of several yet unseen subatomic particles.[5] His theory has been constructed by "filling in" the symmetry gaps in a projection of a hyper-dimensional pattern – 248-dimensional to be precise (!) – known to mathematicians as the "E_8 Lie group." The E_8 Lie group is often considered the most beautiful geometric structure in mathematics, 2D projections of which resemble mandalas.[6] As Lisi speculated, "the geometry of this shape could describe everything about how the universe works."[7] Again, there is no reason in principle to believe that nature should conform to an E_8 Lie group or any other symmetrical pattern, yet the intuition that it does has a strong hold on science. We seem hardwired to believe that truth is somehow associated with the beauty – that is, the symmetries

– of abstract patterns. When our models of nature break the regularity of the pattern, an inner voice screams to us that such models must be wrong or incomplete. The existence of this intuition alone is, from a psychological perspective, intriguing. The empirical fact that it has, time and again, been demonstrated to hold is nothing short of extraordinary. The intuition may reflect a resonance of inner theater in regular awareness, the empirical validation of which may confirm the applicability of inner theater insights to consensus reality.

Now, the idea we are entertaining here goes deeper and is far more radical than the current epistemological status of abstract symmetries in science. While physicists have looked for, and found, abstract patterns in their mathematical *descriptions* of the behavior of matter and energy – matter and energy being assumed objective realities – what we are entertaining here is the possibility that *matter and energy are themselves but patterns of thought*. In other words, the idea being considered is that objectivity – or realism – is a fallacy; that the whole of reality is fundamentally subjective: a projection of patterns of pure thought onto a canvas of space-time that itself exists but in a transpersonal form of mind. What we are exploring is the idea that *everything is in and of mind*. Such idea entails an ultimate reduction of all things to an ultimate level of abstraction.

Reductionism is a canon of scientific thought entailing that any object or phenomenon can be explained by simpler objects or phenomena. This way, science explains a human being in terms of organs; organs in terms of tissues; tissues in terms of cells; cells in terms of molecules; molecules in terms of atoms; atoms in terms of subatomic particles; and, tentatively, subatomic particles in terms of vibrating "strings."[8] *The problem with the assumption of objectivity in the framework of reductionism is that, for as long as a "thing" is assumed to have objective reality, it begs to be explained in terms of other "things" that also have objective reality. This is an unending circularity. One never quite gets to the heart of the matter* (no pun intended). In practice, one cannot explain one thing in terms of another ad infinitum. The game must stop at some point and it currently stops at the "strings." They are then considered "fundamental building blocks of nature" – technical jargon for "we haven't got a clue what they are." From the level of complexity of "strings" up towards organisms, all things can be explained in terms of their *relative differences*, or relationships. This way, a given subatomic particle corresponds to a given vibration mode of the string, like a note. Another subatomic particle then corresponds to another note, different from the first one. We can then talk about two different notes because the vibration frequency of one is, for instance, higher than that of the other, *whatever the underlying strings may be, so long as they can be said to vibrate*. Once a library of subatomic particles is established based on the relative differences of vibration modes – and by abstracting away the underlying nature of whatever vibrates – a virtually unending variety of molecules, cells, tissues, organs, and living beings can be coherently derived from it. Science can then tentatively explain all things on the basis of their relative differences, without ever tackling the glaring ontological hole at the bottom of the chain of complexity: *just what is the stuff that vibrates to begin with?*

The possibility that suggests itself is that, at the very bottom of the chain, there is just *mind*. The ultimate reduction step is not towards another *thing*, or another *object*, but towards elemental thought patterns, subjective by their very nature and externalized in the shared canvas of space-time just like a vivid dream is externalized in the private canvas of the psyche. These elemental thought patterns may have encoded in themselves the seeds of all variability, dynamics, complexity, and relationships of manifested reality. They may be the proto-minded soldiers, obedient to conscious intent and direction, whose very coalescing bodies, like atoms, form the constructs projected onto space-time. This idea would solve the so-called "hard problem of consciousness" in one fell swoop by placing consciousness at the basis of nature. Consciousness would no longer need to be reduced to – that is, explained by – anything else, but would rather be primary. It would be the one underlying "stuff" of nature out of which everything else gains its existence according to a formidable chain of complex interactions.

Through these complex interactions, the elemental thought patterns seen in and by themselves in inner theater may coalesce into the world we see in consensus reality. There may be little left of the original patterns at the level of complexity our ordinary perception operates. However, the data from subjective exploration also suggests that nature is fractal across its different levels; in other words, that the fundamental patterns of nature repeat themselves at all scales. If this is true, then we may expect to see fractal resonances of those now invisible, fundamental thought patterns in our macroscopic world. Naturally, this would imply that nature is itself fractal. And indeed, in his visionary book "The Fractal Geometry of Nature,"[9] Benoit Mandelbrot has shown that many aspects of nature, from galaxy clusters to coastlines, manifest the property of self-similarity associated with fractals. Similar fractal patterns can be observed in phenomena as distinct as the formation of mountains, river networks, lightning, and the growth of pulmonary blood vessels. To this day, scientists continue to uncover more and more aspects of nature that are fractal, compiling a growing list that already includes clouds, plants, mollusks, mountains, and even earthquakes. See Figure 8 for a striking example of a living fractal.

The influence of elemental thought patterns in consensus reality may be exerted non-locally at multiple levels of complexity – from the microscopic, to the macroscopic, to the social, to the cosmological – for those thought patterns are fractal. Their self-similar structure, with multiple nested levels, may interact with reality at multiple scales and also in a self-

Figure 8. The Romanesco broccoli, a striking example of a living fractal. Notice the self-similarity of the pattern at multiple scales.

similar manner. At large scales, these interactions would entail noticeable *correlations* that we would interpret as a form of non-local causation. After all, a single elemental thought pattern, fractally reflected at, say, a cosmological scale, may have instantaneous causal efficacy over large distances in space. From the point of view of science, this effect would be construed to violate local realism; that is, to contradict the idea that objective causal influences cannot propagate instantaneously through space. Sure enough, the phenomenon of quantum entanglement, predicted in quantum theory and now demonstrated experimentally many times over, does seem to violate local realism. As a team of scientists stated in the scientific journal *Nature*, "experiments with entangled pairs of particles have amply confirmed these quantum predictions, thus rendering local realistic theories untenable."[10]

Notice that, by speculating that reality may be a kind of dream, I am not attempting to rob reality of its intrinsic characteristics – of its concreteness, autonomy, or endurance. No. Instead, what I am trying to say is that the qualities of a dream, like its relative (lack of) concreteness, endurance, and autonomy, span ranges that may go beyond what we normally attribute to them; that dreams can take on qualities we normally reserve to our conception of consensus reality. In other words, dreams could perhaps be a lot more concrete, enduring, and autonomous than we normally think. And yet, I am also speculating that reality is fundamentally subjective and mental in nature; that although its felt concreteness is real – as far as the perceptual qualities we associate with "concreteness" – such concreteness cannot be construed to imply objectivity. Reality is a dream because dreams and mentality can be more like reality than we thought possible, without losing their inherently subjective nature.

At this point, you may ask: If reality is a product of the imagination, then why can we not make of it whatever we want?

Indeed, it is an obvious fact about reality that we cannot individually control it at will. Notice, however, that if reality is indeed imagined, then it is necessarily the compound result of multiple imaginations at work simultaneously. Though reality may be fundamentally grounded in our mental processes, since there are many of us acting consciously at any moment in time, no individual imagination could independently determine the resulting outcome. What each one of us perceives may, therefore, be radically different from what we are each trying to imagine. This indeed may lie at the heart of our overwhelming tendency to believe in objectivity, for an autonomous physics seems to explain our apparent lack of control over reality. Still, our laws of physics, objective as they may seem, may be simply the emerging result of a kind of synchronization mechanism by means of which the output of individual minds combine together to form consensus reality.

If this hypothesis is true, then our cognition and ability to conceive of the mechanisms of reality are, by construction, self-fulfilling. After all, what we imagine is but what we can conceive. *Our imagination is a reflection of our cognitive models and expectations.* So the reality we project onto the fabric of space-time is the reality we are capable of conceiving and expecting. This way, there may be no fundamental difference between a standalone truth and the result of a self-fulfilling expectation. In fact, perhaps all realities are necessarily self-fulfilled, in the sense that there must be enough momentum in consciously expecting such realities for them to actually coalesce into existence from the underlying elemental thought forms. All truth may necessarily be the result of self-fulfilling beliefs, conceptions, and expectations, *even the truth of the known laws of physics.*

As a matter of fact, the role of expectation in the execution of physics experiments is something that may not be well enough understood. Biochemist Dr. Rupert Sheldrake claimed to have once carried out a survey of the use of blind experimental techniques in different branches of science.[11] The idea of a blind experiment is that nobody involved, not even the researchers themselves, know certain critical information about the tests being done, the knowledge of which could otherwise influence the results through personal biases. Blind techniques are often used in the medical sciences so neither patients nor evaluating doctors know, until the study is complete, which patient received what treatment. The goal is to prevent the largely unexplained placebo effect, whereby the patient's expectations alone lead to significant health improvements, from polluting the results.[12] Sheldrake's survey concluded that, *in the physical sciences – physics and chemistry – none of the studies surveyed employed blind techniques.* In other words, the researchers involved knew exactly, *while carrying out the experiments*, which observations would confirm their hypotheses and which would not. They knew exactly what to expect or hope for. If our speculations are correct, this could have directly influenced the results. Would it not be prudent to assume, just in case, that something analogous to the mysterious placebo effect might play a role in the physical sciences as well? After all, the placebo effect has been empirically observed in the medical sciences with overwhelming and growing consistency.[13] Since we do not yet have complete knowledge of the causal mechanisms behind it, is it safe to assume that the placebo effect is restricted to the medical field alone? As Sheldrake asked, "do you get different results in a physics experiment if you do it blind compared with doing it with the usual open conditions, where you know which sample is which?"[14]

In speculating about all these ideas, we must not close our eyes to obvious aspects of the world around us. Indeed, while the Pattern unfolding from the "Source," as observed during my own subjective exploration, was perfect in its symmetry and regularity, we live in a world that has clear asymmetries and irregularities. We live in a world of *entropy* – that is, of *dis*order – a concept totally alien to the perfect organization and undiminishing order of the Source. Therefore, if consensus reality is but a partial projection of the Pattern unfolding from the Source, how could asymmetries, irregularities, and entropy have arisen in our universe? At first sight, that seems impossible, except for one sleight of hand: *if the creative intent of the Source is fragmented in such a way that each fragment becomes a relatively independent causal agency in the composition of reality, then the coherence of the underlying creative force is broken and a degree of disorder is introduced into the system.*

It is well known in the field of dynamical systems that even small disturbances in the coherence of a system can lead to significant and growing irregularities in its global behavior. We will see a dramatic example of this in the next chapter. In chaotic systems, so-called "strange attractors" can condense and amplify small fluctuations in the system's regular dynamics, allowing irregularities to take hold and grow.[15] We know that our universe is one such a system: in our cosmological past, gravity clumped matter around supposedly random fluctuations at the quantum scale to form the irregularities that ultimately became stars, planets, you, and me.[16] So there are two processes at play here: the first is a process that introduces irregularities in the system; the second is a process capable of amplifying these irregularities. I speculate that, in the hyperdimensional fabric of space-time that transcends and encompasses our consensus reality, the first process is associated with the fragmentation of conscious intent arising from the clumping up of consciousness in different focal points. Such fragmentation of intentionality breaks, at some level, the coherence of the underlying Pattern. This, in turn, introduces local disturbances that are then amplified, thereby creating the variety of irregular phenomena we perceive in our realm of reality. In the slice of hyper-dimensional space-time corresponding to consensus reality, quantum chance is perhaps a reminiscent echo of these disturbances. And the critical role of quantum chance in our universe has been eloquently highlighted by Seth Lloyd, when he wrote that "chance is a crucial element of the language of nature. Every roll of the quantum dice injects a few more bits of detail into the world. As these details accumulate, they form the seeds for all the variety of the universe. Every tree, branch, leaf, cell, and strand of DNA owes its particular form to some past toss of the quantum dice."[17]

As suggested by mathematician Ralph Abraham,[18] *chaos, or apparent disorder, is the fertile ground where novelty germinates.* Chaos is a necessary condition for unpredictable, previously unknown behaviors and phenomenality to arise in a system. Therefore, if the Source of creation is orderly and harmonious, chaos has to somehow emerge out of what is intrinsically orderly, so novelty can be experienced. This may be another clue to why consciousness seems to clump up in distinct focal points that then go down the path of individual experience. Disorder may be produced out of order through a trick: a decoupling of different, orderly segments of the underlying mechanisms of reality that causes these segments to fall out of step with one another and lose their global coherence. These creative, conscious segments of the whole can now independently project different versions of reality onto a common fabric of space-time – based on their own, separate, local contexts – leading to largely unpredictable, novel, emergent combinations. The relatively disorderly reality we actually experience may emerge out of a complex amalgamation of these different projections. This way, *the fragmentation of conscious intent may allow the universe to generate, out of itself, something novel and unknown to itself.*

Perhaps only in inner theater can we tap into the raw chaos of Kandinsky scintillae and build compositions of elemental thought patterns that do not conform to learned belief systems or culturally sanctioned worldviews. Maybe only there are we able to break free from the self-reinforcing and repetitive stories of consensus reality; to see past the haze of habit and convention; to cognize the *truth* in all its naked glory, unclothed by culture. Our ability to visit and work in the unpolluted, private canvas of our imaginations may lie at the basis not only of creativity, but of wisdom and of our potential to evolve as individuals and as a society.

Chapter 12

Summing it all up with a structured metaphor

Mathematician Ralph Abraham once said of non-ordinary states of consciousness: "Any models that we can build, verbal, visual, or mathematical, are feeble compared to the experience itself. On the other hand, this experience is within all, [...] so the tiniest resonance from the feeblest model may suffice to excite, as poetry excites emotion, spirit. The essence of communication is to have a compact representation of an experience that's infinitely complex. [...] Representations restricted to verbal mode alone might be too feeble to excite by resonance, the similar state."[1] It is inspired by these words that I now set out to achieve an ambitious goal: that of finding and conveying a simple, coherent, and holistic representation of personal experiences that have been formidably complex and nuanced. And this representation must not be grounded in language, as the discussions of the previous chapters have been, but must instead add a new and *synthesizing* perspective to our story.

The tool we will use is mathematics. But fear not: there will be no equations or complex notations whatsoever. All I will use to elicit your intuition are pretty pictures, which happen to be mathematically generated. Nonetheless, if you are really uncomfortable with any kind of formal thinking at all, you may skip this chapter, for it adds no new information to what has already been discussed. It is simply an attempt to consolidate and further illustrate previously introduced ideas. On the other hand, for those of you whose minds resonate with formal logic, the discussion that follows provides an integrative perspective, in the framework of which many ideas will come together. It will also allow us to study, by means of computer simulations of a toy dreamed-up reality, some of the implications of the ideas discussed in the preceding chapters. For those eager to dive into all the mathematical details, I provide further information in the appendix.

At this point, an important disclaimer should be made. It may be tempting to interpret the upcoming pages as an attempt by me to model reality according to an outlandish and unsubstantiated set of premises. No, I am not *that* naïvely ambitious. My intent is solely to construct a *metaphor* of my own interpretation of the subjective experiences I underwent, in the hope of communicating that interpretation with clarity and of deriving some of its implications. The difference between these two things is crucial: while a model of reality starts from objective observations of facts, seeking to articulate these observations in a framework of cause and effect, the metaphor I seek starts from my own intuitions. What you will find in the pages that follow is an exfoliation of ideas, not a model of facts. After all, this is not a book with a thesis. Moreover, as any metaphor, the one described in the coming paragraphs is not perfect: while most of its elements accurately correspond to my intuitions, others do not and may even contradict aspects of those intuitions.

Before we get started, we need to lay some simple foundations and terminology so you will be able to interpret the upcoming pictures. The first term we need to get acquainted with is "cellular automaton," a mathematical construct well studied over the past several decades.[2] Though the name "cellular automaton" may sound intimidating, there is actually nothing complicated about the idea. In fact, Figure 9 is an example of a simple cellular automaton. For now, look only at the upper row of squares in the figure. Each square is called a "cell." The cellular automaton is the set of all seven cells shown in Figure 9. Each cell may be either black or white. We say that a cell can have one of two different "states" at any moment in

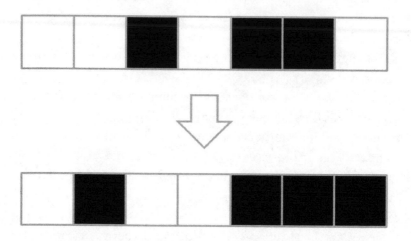

Figure 9. A simple example of a 1-dimensional cellular automaton showing two subsequent generations of states.

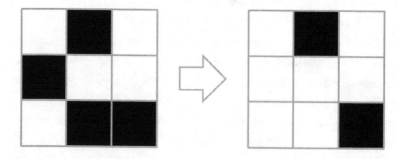

Figure 10. A simple example of a 2-dimensional cellular automaton showing two subsequent generations of states.

time: black or white. Many authors prefer the more dramatic terminology "alive" or "dead" for the two possible states of a cell. That is fine too.

Each cell has two neighboring cells: one to the left and the other to the right. Together, the cell and its neighbors form a "neighborhood." Clearly, each cell has its own neighborhood and the neighborhoods of different cells partially overlap. We assume that the topology of the cellular automaton is a ring. This way, the left neighbor of the leftmost cell is the rightmost cell. Similarly, the right neighbor of the rightmost cell is the leftmost cell. In other words, the row of cells "wraps around" forming a closed ring, though that is not shown in Figure 9. There, instead, the ring is shown "cut" and "stretched open" for ease of depiction. Because the cellular automaton contains a single row of cells – that is, a single dimension (left-right) – we say that it is a 1-dimensional automaton.

Now, the key point is this: the state of each cell in the cellular automaton changes over time, depending on its own current state and the current states of its neighbors. In other words, the next state of each cell depends on the current configuration of states in the cell's own neighborhood. It is this that renders cellular automata useful tools for studying dynamical systems. In fact, it has been suggested by scientists that the universe itself may operate like a cellular automaton of cosmic proportions.[3] On a more practical scale, cellular automata have been success-fully used for modeling a variety of physical systems.[4] Clearly, thus, cellular automata are good vehicles for a metaphor of reality, which is what we are attempting to construct.

The set of all cell states in the automaton at a given moment in time is called a "generation." The way the state of the cells changes from one generation to the next, over time, is deter-mined by a so-called "state transition rule." The state transition rule must specify the next state of a cell depending on the current configuration of states in the cell's neighborhood. Here is a simple example of a state transition rule: the next state of each cell becomes black (alive) if the current state of exactly one of the cell's respective two neighbors is black; in all other cases, it becomes white (dead). In Figure 9, the lower row of cells shows the new generation of the cellular automaton when exactly this state transition rule is applied to the generation represented in the upper row. Have a look and check it for yourself, so you get some intuition about how cellular automata work. Do not forget: what you see is actually a ring cut open, so all cells have two neighbors.

This may all be sounding very abstract to you at this point. But bear with me a little longer, for the purpose and usefulness of all this is going to become clear shortly. The path we will be pursuing is, first, to port the intuitions of subjective exploration onto the framework of cellular automata. Then we will simulate the evolution of these automata on a computer, thereby gener-ating the promised pretty pictures, to see what it tells us about the implications of those intuitions.

As mentioned earlier, the cellular automaton in Figure 9 has a single dimension (left-right). However, we could add an extra dimension by stacking the representations of subsequent gener-ations on top of each other. For instance, in Figure 9, by stacking the rows corresponding to each of the two consecutive genera-tions on top of one another, we add the dimension of time to the automaton (past-future). We will come back to this point later on. For now, let us look at the possibility of adding an extra dimension of *space* to the automaton, as opposed to a dimension of time.

Figure 10 illustrates a 2-dimensional automaton where, in addition to the left-right dimension, a top-down dimension is added. So now, instead of a row, the cellular automaton entails a three by three array of cells, each cell being either dead (white) or alive (black). The same, simple state transition rule discussed above is applied to produce the next generation of the automaton: from the generation on the left to the generation on the right of Figure 10, a cell becomes or stays alive if, and only if, exactly one of its neighbors is alive. Notice that each cell has now four neighbors: to the left, right, up, and down. Diagonally adjacent cells, in this case, do not count as neighbors. Notice also that, again, we assume that the cellular automaton "wraps around" in both directions. In other words, the upper neighbor of a cell in the top row is the cell occupying the same column but in the bottom row. Similarly, the left neighbor of a cell in the first (leftmost) column is the cell occupying the same row but in the last (rightmost) column. Technically, the topology of such automaton is said to be "toroidal;" that is, doughnut-shaped. The representation in Figure 10 basically corresponds to the doughnut being "cut open" and "unwrapped" to form a flat square.

As the states of the automaton change from one generation to the next, new configurations of black and white cells in the 2-dimensional array are produced. Each of these generations thus corresponds to a frame in a kind of black & white movie, each cell corresponding to a pixel in the respective movie frames. By displaying the frames in rapid succession, one can actually see an animation of the evolution of the cellular automaton's states. Artists have used this possibility to amazing effect, simulating not only physical phenomena but the appearance of life itself.[5] The result is that we are now dealing with a total of three dimensions – two in space and one in time – namely: left-right, top-down, and past-future. However, since a book page has only two dimensions, it becomes now impossible to display all these successive generations in a single picture. Instead, we will need to show them side by side, as separate frames.

Our ordinary experience is that we live in a 4-dimensional world with three dimensions of space (left-right, up-down, back-forth) and one of time (past-future). When I suggested that the Source unfolded in a *hyper*-dimensional realm, the implication was that such realm would need to span more than the four dimensions mentioned, which is impossible to represent graphically. Therefore, inspired by Prof. Abraham, we will use a dramatic simplification: we will attempt to represent the unfolding of the Source in only two dimensions, so the representation can be printed on a page of this book. To do that, we will use a 2-dimensional cellular automaton, like that illustrated in Figure 10, but with a more sophisticated state transition rule.

In the 2-dimensional cellular automaton under consideration, each cell has four neighbors. Therefore, each neighborhood comprises five cells: the center cell and the four cells orthogonally adjacent to it (technically, this is called a "von Neumann neighborhood of range 1"). Since each of these five cells can assume one of two possible states (alive or dead), there are $2^5 =$ 32 different possible state configurations in a neighborhood. Therefore, the state transition rule must determine, for each of these thirty-two possibilities, whether the center cell goes dead (white) or alive (black) in the subsequent generation.

Let us now start building the metaphor itself. Each of these thirty-two possibilities corresponds to a *pattern* both in space (that is, the current configuration of black and white cells in the neighborhood) and in time (the implied color of the neighborhood's center cell in the next generation). A key intuition about the unfolding of the Source was its radial symmetry; that is, the idea that the unfolding Pattern would not change when subjected to a rotation. For instance, a square is symmetric to rotations of 90 degrees, in that if you rotate a square by 90 degrees you get the same square again. Let us thus require the same kind of symmetry of our 32 possible neighborhood patterns: let us require that the state transition rule be such that all 90-degree rotations of a given neighborhood pattern lead to the same next state for the neighborhood's center cell. With this requirement, we just need to specify the state transition rule for the twelve neighborhood patterns shown in Figure 11. All other

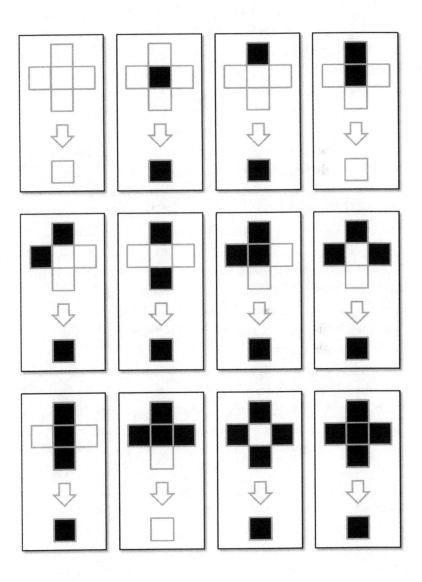

Figure 11. The twelve neighborhood patterns used in the cellular automaton metaphor of the Source. The cell state shown under each arrow represents the next state of the respective pattern's center cell.

possible neighborhood patterns can be derived by 90-degree rotations of the ones shown. Therefore, since the state transition rule must specify the next state of the center cell for each of these twelve patterns, we have 2^{12} = 4,096 possible state transition rules.

In the days immediately following the third experiment, for some reason unclear to me, I felt compelled to experiment with some of these 4,096 different possibilities and investigate the evolution of the corresponding cellular automata. I did not know what I was looking for until I stumbled upon one particular state transition rule. Never mind this mild unlikelihood. The particular rule I stumbled upon is illustrated in Figure 11 by means of the cell pointed to by the arrow below each of the twelve patterns shown. The color of that cell represents the next state of the center cell given the corresponding neighborhood pattern. This way, the state transition rule shown in Figure 11 may read as follows (from the left-upper corner to the lower-right corner): if the center cell is dead and all its four neighbors are dead, the center cell remains dead; if the center cell is alive and all its four neighbors are dead, the center cell remains alive; if the center cell is dead but a single one of its four neighbors is alive, then the center cell goes alive; ... if the center cell is alive and all its four neighbors are also alive, the center cell remains alive. Notice that each and every cell in the cellular automaton is the center cell of its respective neighborhood – different neighborhoods partially overlapping – so the state transition rule fully specifies how the state of each cell evolves over time.

Okay, if you have followed it up until this point, it is downhill from here. What I now did was to define a cellular automaton in the form of a square array wherein the number of rows and columns was a power of two plus one cells (for instance, $2^8 + 1$ = 257 cells). As I found out later, the effect described below works *only* in case the array is defined this way; another mild unlikelihood. I initially set all cells in the array as dead (white), except the one cell at the very center of the array, which I initially set as alive (black). Thereafter, I recursively applied the state transition rule illustrated in Figure 11. What then happened was amazing.

In Figure 12, a few frames of the evolution of the resulting cellular automaton are shown. Each frame corresponds to a generation of the automaton, from the 32nd to the 512th generation, at intervals of thirty-two generations. As it can be seen in the figure, the single live cell at the center of the array begins to unfold fractally into an amazing, composite, triangular-themed Pattern. The static frames in Figure 12 do not capture the amazing dynamics one sees when watching an animation of the cellular automaton in action. As this composite, unfolding Pattern reaches the boundaries of the array, it folds back onto itself. The edges of the unfolding Pattern proceed towards the center of the array *without interfering with the outgoing segments of itself*, as if moving in a hyper-dimensional plane that is actually not part of the cellular automaton algorithm at all. The effect is extraordinary and profoundly counterintuitive from a mathematical perspective.

As the evolution of the automaton continues, the now incoming and outgoing segments of the unfolding Pattern conflate into new and surprising fractal rearrangements. New form is created everywhere in the array, with surprising harmony and coherence. Though the basic triangular theme persists throughout, triangular arrangements with different configurations blossom out of other triangular arrangements at various points of the array, in a seemingly continuous rebirthing of new shapes out of prior shapes. Eventually, as we can see when comparing the 8th and 16th frames shown in Figure 12, the evolution of the automaton returns to a previous configuration and then starts repeating itself in a cycle. This way, the automaton never stops. It continues on in an open-ended rebirthing of fractal form; a perpetual, continuous, and

Figure 12. Evolution of the cellular automaton metaphor of the Source. Each of the sixteen frames shown corresponds to a different generation of states.

recursive morphogenesis *that requires nothing from the outside*. As far as the automaton is concerned, there might just as well be no outside. *It is entirely self-sufficient in its potential for creation.* Indeed, all of what is seen in Figure 12 is simply the result of the recursive application of the basic rules shown in Figure 11 to a single live cell at the center of a 2-dimensional array. Nothing more. No intervention is required once the system is set in motion. However, although the fractal never stops unfolding, *novelty is limited*: no truly new forms can be produced beyond the point when the cycle starts repeating itself.

This is the metaphor I sought for the Source. The neighborhood patterns of Figure 11 are a metaphor for the elemental thought patterns underlying reality. The single live cell at the center of the array is a metaphor for the elusive home of the Source and its initial creative impetus. By recursively applying the elemental thought patterns to Itself, the Source unfolds into an endless, hyper-dimensional creation of a higher-level, composite thought Pattern wherein the dynamics of the entire creation are completely encoded in the original, elemental thought patterns themselves. In the composite, unfolding thought Pattern represented in Figure 12, the original forms of the elemental thought patterns of Figure 11 are dispersed. For any mathematically naïve observer watching the evolution of the unfolding Pattern in Figure 12, it would be nearly impossible to infer that the elemental thought patterns of Figure 11 were actually the underlying reality of everything he or she was observing; that there was *nothing* more to what is seen in Figure 12 than the recursive application, or the *unfolding*, of the space-time patterns of Figure 11.

The fractal nature of the unfolding Pattern can be more clearly seen in Figure 13, which is a higher resolution version of the fourth frame shown in Figure 12. At multiple levels, the arrangements of triangles repeat themselves self-similarly. This way, a version of the entire unfolding Pattern can be seen in

Figure 13. A frame corresponding to a generation of states of the cellular automaton metaphor of the Source. Notice the fractal self-similarities of the pattern.

smaller parts of itself. Different segments of the unfolding Pattern can be seen repeated again and again, at different magnifications and orientations, without ever breaking the harmonious symmetry of the whole. It may be worthwhile that you spend some time observing Figure 13 to clearly see what I mean here. That figure alone is fertile ground for many discoveries, if you know how to look. Intuitively, it may feel like a wonder that all the complexity and sophistication seen in Figure 13 are but a composite reflection, or an amalgamation in space and time, of the simple patterns shown in Figure 11. Notice also that, just like the elemental thought patterns in Figure 11, the entire unfolding Pattern shown in Figure 13 remains exactly the same if rotated by 90 degrees. This is like a fractal resonance of characteristics of the elemental thought patterns on their own compound manifestation, but at a higher level of complexity.

The coherence of the unfolding Pattern depends on the *strict* application of the state transition rule represented in Figure 11 to *all* cells of the cellular automaton array. Any disruption in this process breaks its coherence and eventually leads to a total breakdown of the unfolding Pattern. Indeed, in Figure 14 the same cellular automaton evolution of Figure 12 is displayed, but this time *a single cell* (out of 66,049) at the center of the left-upper quadrant of the array has been fixed at a dead state, regardless of the application of the state transition rule. In other words, a single cell is stuck in "white," while the other 66,048 operate normally. The result of this minimal disruption is seen starting from the 5th frame shown in Figure 14. Notice that, eventually, that small disruption causes the entire unfolding Pattern to collapse into *chaos* and *entropy*. Instead of forever repeating itself in a regular, predictable, fractal manner, the unfolding Pattern dissolves into unpredictable, non-repeating noise.

But my intuition was that the Source continuously unfolds in perfect regularity. It never breaks down into irregular, chaotic behavior. Therefore, given that chaos – that is, unpredictable

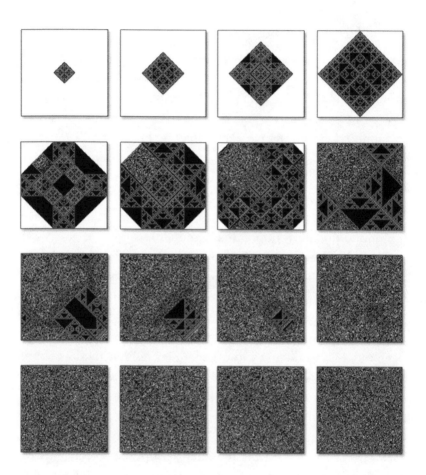

Figure 14. Evolution of the cellular automaton metaphor of the Source. Unlike in Figure 12, this time a single cell at the center of the left-upper quadrant of the array has been fixed at a dead state. Notice the ensuing chaos.

irregularities – seems to be a prerequisite for *novelty*, there must be another way in our present metaphor to represent how novelty is continuously created.

And indeed there is. The way to do it can be derived from the following observation: chaos, disorder, and entropy can be attested to be facts *only of manifested reality*. The intuition of the underlying reality of nature, according at least to my own experiences, does not encompass chaos. Much to the contrary: the realm of the Source seems to be the ultimate embodiment of *perfect order and structure*. So it is not in the plane of the Source, represented in Figures 12 and 13, that we should look for chaos. Instead, it is in another plane – that of *manifested reality* – that we should expect to find it. And then, somehow, the perfect order of the Source must transmute into a fertile ground for novelty when projected onto that plane of manifestation.

How do we bring a plane of manifested reality into our cellular automaton metaphor? The first thing to consider is that, from the experiences of subjective exploration, it appears that the world of consensus reality is a lower-dimensional world than the plane of the Source. So this should be reflected in our metaphor. Given that our representation of the plane of the Source has used two dimensions of space, we are left with only one alternative: to represent the plane of manifested reality with a single dimension of space. That brings us back to a 1-dimensional cellular automaton structure like that illustrated in Figure 9.

However, the state transition rule of this 1-dimensional automaton should be better thought out now. A key intuition from subjective exploration has been that consensus reality is a kind of amalgamation, or constrained synchronization, of the images projected by different consciousnesses onto a shared fabric of space-time. We can capture this idea in the state transition rule of the 1-dimensional automaton in a relatively simple way: we can have each cell obey its own, private state transition rule. In other words, each cell now seeks to determine how its own state should change over time, in a idiosyncratic manner. As a metaphor for the individual intent of each cell, we can randomly initialize their corresponding state transition rules. Each cell, with its own, private, randomly initialized state transition rule then becomes a metaphor for an independent, individual consciousness. What we now have to add to the scheme is the idea that manifested reality is somehow synchronized across different consciousnesses.

To represent that, we can do the following: let us imagine that the individual state transition rule of a cell not only influences how its own state changes, but also how the states of its two neighbors change. In other words, let us imagine that the intent of a cell is projected out onto what happens to its neighbors, according to the worldview – that is, the state transition rule – of that cell. For instance, if a cell "looks around" and finds its two neighbors to be black while the cell itself is white, its worldview may dictate that it should turn black in the next generation. *But it then also tries to project its own worldview onto its neighbors, by "expecting" that both neighboring cells will also turn black when they are white and their respective neighbors are black.* Its neighbors will be doing the same thing: each will be trying to determine its own future state according to its respective worldview – that is, its private state transition rule – and projecting that worldview onto its neighbors. So which worldview wins for which cell? The intuition from subjective exploration is that this synchronization of different worldviews is the mechanism by means of which a common, shared reality emerges.

While we need to keep our metaphor simple, we do not want to oversimplify it to the point where it becomes trivial. So let us do as follows. There are three different causal influences in determining the next state of each cell: the worldview of the cell itself and those of its two neighbors. Let us say that the worldview of a cell has twice the weight of those of its neighbors in determining the cell's own next state. This is a metaphor for the fact that force fields in our universe are stronger over shorter distances. So we basically have three "voters:" one of them (the cell itself) casting two identical "votes" and the other two (the cell's neighbors) each casting a single vote. Since the next state of the cell can only be black or white, each vote can be either for black or for white. A majority-rule is the obvious way to decide which state actually manifests from the projected worldviews of the three cells involved. For instance, if three or four of the votes are for "black," the cell becomes black in the next generation; analogously for "white." However, in case of a tie – that is, when both neighbors vote for one state while the cell itself votes for the opposite state, resulting in a two-two vote – the next state is then determined by a "cross-dimensional influence" from the Source, as will be described below. This determination of an element of manifested reality from outside the system, when no favored direction is consciously chosen from within the system, can be seen as a metaphor for the quantum chance underlying nature.

We are almost there. Only two extra elements are now missing from our metaphor of manifested reality. Bear with me a little longer.

When we say that a cell only looks at itself and its two neighbors to form its image of what should happen next in its immediate surroundings, this works as a metaphor for the fact that our own perception of reality is limited to our immediate vicinity. After all, we can only see, hear, or otherwise perceive that which is near to us. Our five senses are local by their very nature. However, when we limit the "range of perception" of a cell solely to itself and its two neighbors, all of which have randomized state transition rules, the result is absolute disorder. Each cell tries to project its own random worldview around itself. Its neighbors do the same thing. Although the majority view wins, all contributors to that view act randomly, so the end result is also pure randomness.

That is not quite how our own consensus reality seems to work. Although we do live in a world of entropy and disorder, that world also has elements of order and structure: crystals and living organisms, for example. In fact, it seems that it is precisely those regular and structured elements that seem to give meaning to the dance of manifested existence, for pure randomness is meaningless. To capture this in our metaphor, we need to link up the 1-dimensional plane of manifested reality to the 2-dimensional plane of the unfolding Pattern. In other words, *we need to extend the range of perception of each cell – each cell being a metaphor for an individual conscious entity with private intent – to a projection of the Source.* In our metaphor, it must be the unfolding regularity of the Source that injects order and structure into what would otherwise be an entirely meaningless plane of manifestation. Similarly, it must be the potential *dis*order of the plane of manifestation – originating from the independent worldviews of its cells – that introduces *novelty* in the hierarchy of all planes.

To operationalize these concepts, let us look at Figure 15. Two planes are shown: that of manifested reality on top and, below, a plane containing a 1-dimensional projection of the unfolding Pattern illustrated in Figure 12. There are many different ways we could define such a projection, but the simplest is to simply take a single row or column from the unfolding Pattern. That is indeed what I did, and I arbitrarily chose a row half way between the center of the array and its boundary. Since the evolution of the unfolding Pattern seems to flow cyclically across all rows and columns anyway, an arbitrary choice here is reasonable. Both planes illustrated in Figure 15 comprise a single row of cells. The other rows of cells drawn in the background, with dashed lines, represent the previous generations of states of these cells as such states evolved over time, according to the arrow of time shown.

In the plane of manifestation shown in Figure 15, a cell is

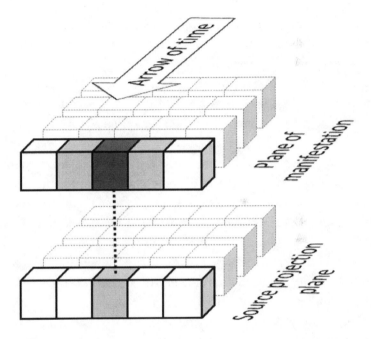

Figure 15. Diagram of the relationship between the 1-dimensional cellular automaton representing the plane of manifestation and the Source projection plane. Notice that a cell neighborhood in the plane of manifestation (represented by the gray cells) spans across planes.

represented in dark grey. This cell is just a reference cell: the entire discussion that follows applies equally to all other cells in that plane. In lighter grey, the reference cell's two neighbors are shown. But now the corresponding cell in the underlying Source projection plane – it too represented in lighter gray – is also made part of the reference cell's neighborhood. In other words, *the range of perception of the conscious entity represented by the reference cell now extends beyond its immediate vicinity in the plane of manifestation and into the underlying Source projection plane*. In our metaphor, this perception by the reference cell of a corresponding cell in the Source projection plane could be seen as a kind of cross-dimensional, perhaps instinctive, extra-sensorial perception – or intuition. In addition, and as briefly mentioned earlier, we also do the following: not only will each neighborhood cross-dimensionally encompass a cell from the Source projection plane; in case of a tied vote, the next state of this cell will also determine the reference cell's next state. In our metaphor, this would correspond to a structured, patterned control of the "row of the quantum dice" when the conscious entities in the plane of manifestation are unable to make an unambiguous choice about which reality should manifest.

Let us now elaborate on the last element we need in our metaphor, before we run the resulting simulations and interpret the images produced. This last, missing element is *learning*. As we have seen, each cell in the plane of manifestation of Figure 15 operates in the following way: first, it looks at its own current state, the current states of its two neighboring cells, and the current state of the corresponding cell in the Source projection plane; then, on the basis of these observations and of its own, initially random worldview – that is, its state transition rule – it determines what its next state should be and projects that determination not only at itself, but also at its two neighbors. Since each neighbor will be doing the same thing, the next state of each cell is determined by the "majority vote" across the three different expectations of reality being projected at the position of that cell, the cell's own expectation having twice the weight of those of its neighbors. If the vote is tied, the cell's next state is then determined entirely by the Source projection plane. What we will now do is the following: once the winning cell states emerge out of this "voting" system, each cell observes what *actually* happened to itself and its neighbors in the plane of manifestation. In other words, each cell compares the expectations it projected at its surroundings to the reality that *actually* manifested. It may then find that what actually happened is not what it had expected to happen. And here is the crucial point: upon this realization, we program the cell to *learn* from what actually manifested. In other words, each cell adapts its own state transition rule to make it consistent with the cell states actually taken on by itself and its neighbors after the "voting." This way, the initially random state transition rules change over time, conforming to the local reality observed by the respective cells. With this learning, each cell will adjust its own expectations, cognition models, or worldviews – all equivalent words in the context of our metaphor – in accordance with their supposedly objective observations of manifested reality.

Now we are done. All that is left is to actually run the simulations, look at the results, and interpret their implications in the framework of our metaphor.

Figure 16 is divided vertically into three columns. The leftmost column is a top-view of the state evolution of the "plane of manifestation," as explained in Figure 15. The middle column is a top-view of the state evolution of the "Source projection plane," also explained in Figure 15. Finally, the rightmost column shows, through different shades of grey, the differences between the worldviews – that is, state transition rules – of the different cells in the "plane of manifestation." Each worldview is represented by a different shade of grey. In all three cases, the arrow of time points down; that is, each row of

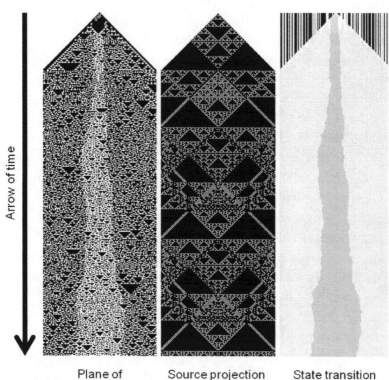

Arrow of time

Plane of manifestation

Source projection plane

State transition rules of the plane of manifestation

Figure 16. An overview of the evolution of states in the plane of manifestation (left) and in the Source projection plane (center), as well as of the different state transition rules operating in the plane of manifestation (right).

the plane of manifestation and the Source projection plane shows the corresponding cell states at a given moment in time. Analogously, each row of the rightmost column codes, with a shade of grey, the state transition rule of each cell of the plane of manifestation at a given moment in time. The idea of the rightmost column is to show how the relative differences between the state transition rules of different cells evolve over time. In other words, the idea is to show how, through *learning in a shared reality*, the initially random state transition rules slowly converge to a common, shared worldview – as represented by the decreasing number of different shades of grey as time goes by.

Let us look at Figure 16 in more detail. We start the simulation at the top. Initially, in the plane of manifestation, a single cell is alive (black) at the center of the corresponding cellular automaton row. All cells are initialized with random state transition rules. *Interestingly, as time goes by, black-filled triangular patterns begin to evolve in the fabric of manifested space-time.* These triangular patterns are an echo of the triangular fractals that concurrently evolve in the Source projection plane. Indeed, although the middle column of Figure 16 is merely a 1-dimensional *projection* of the unfolding Pattern shown in Figure 12, its fractal characteristics are preserved in that projection.

Notice that, although the triangular patterns evolving in the Source projection plane are regular, orderly, and repetitive, their triangular echoes in the plane of manifestation occur at seemingly random locations in both space and time. They also have seemingly random sizes. Finally, and perhaps most importantly, they are *not* repetitive. There is unpredictability and novelty in the plane of manifestation. On the other hand, *there also clearly is structure in the plane of manifestation.* It is not purely random and chaotic. This shows that the influence of the Source projection plane in the state evolution of the plane of manifestation is decisive: it introduces structure and meaning where there would have been none. Notice also that, from the point of view of individual cells in the plane of manifestation, the influence exerted in it by the fractal structures of the Source projection plane seems to be non-local. Indeed, the large triangular patterns evolving in the Source projection plane *instantaneously* affect cells in the plane of manifestation that are far from one another in space. From the point of view of an observer restricted to the plane of manifestation, the correlations entailed would seem to contradict local realism. Notice also that this non-local influence crossing the boundaries of planes is fractal in nature: the same influences may take place at multiple scales of the plane of manifestation, from the microscopic to the macroscopic. The microscopic metaphor would correspond to small fractal triangles in the Source projection plane influencing adjacent cells in the plane of manifestation. The macroscopic metaphor, on the other hand, would correspond to large fractal triangles in the Source projection plane instantaneously influencing cells far from one another in the plane of manifestation. In both cases, the cross-dimensional influence would take on the same pattern: a triangle. As above, so below. The effects of the correlations entailed by the patterns in the Source projection plane would be felt in the plane of manifestation as a kind of Jungian synchronicity[6] – that is, as unexplained "coincidences" – transcending causality.

Notice, in the rightmost column of Figure 16, that initially many different state transition rules – that is, worldviews – are concurrently operating in the plane of manifestation. This is represented by the many shades of grey initially present. Very quickly, however, starting at a point around the middle of the array where there is maximum entropy – that is, variability – of states in the plane of manifestation, the cells start learning. The higher the entropy of states in the plane of manifestation – that is, the more oscillation between black and white states there is – the more different situations the cells experience, thereby adjusting their respective state transition rules accordingly. As that happens, the cells quickly converge to common, shared worldviews. As it can easily be seen in Figure 16, after only a few generations only two different worldviews survive, as represented by the two remaining shades of grey.

Cells immersed in their own worldview – that is, cells surrounded by other cells that have the exact same state transition rule – find complete consistency between their own expectations and what actually manifests. Therefore, they stop learning and their worldview stays stable. In the rightmost column of Figure 16, two clearly defined regions can be seen, each with its own, dominating worldview. *Only at the boundaries between these regions can learning take place.* It is the dialectic tension between conflicting worldviews that leads to the adaptation of cognitive models. Of the two dominating worldviews seen, the one represented by the darker shade of grey clearly wins ground over the other as time goes by. The consequence of this in the plane of manifestation is clearly visible: triangles with more strongly defined edges emerge in the regions where the stronger worldview gains ground.

Perhaps this metaphor can give us some insight into the dynamics of our modern world. In Figure 16, two worldviews survive because communication between adepts of different worldviews can only happen locally. Imagine how quickly these different worldviews would converge to a single, uniform one, if communication could take place remotely, over long distances and bypassing entire regions of space, like what has been possible in our society with technologies like radio, television, and the Internet. In almost no time would the entire world cognize reality in exactly the same way, expecting the exact same things, and the reality manifested in their surroundings would consistently reinforce these expectations. Instead of the clear differences in the plane of manifestation seen in Figure 16, all manifestation would be consistent with one and the same set

147

of state transition rules.

As a matter of fact, *a state transition rule is analogous to the laws of physics*. One state transition rule corresponds to one coherent and internally consistent "physics," so to say. If the physics of our universe could be boiled down to a single equation – that is, one "theory of everything" – then that one equation would correspond to a state transition rule in our metaphor. Indeed, when physicists attempt to model our physics with cellular automata, this is the correspondence they use. Therefore, Figure 16 tells us that, *because of learning in a shared playing field of experience*, what had initially been multiple and contradictory physics, operating concurrently at different points of the plane of manifestation, quickly converges to only two different physics. "Magic" in such a world can only happen at the boundaries of the regions dominated by each respective physics. After all, the phenomena occurring at these boundaries may contradict the cognitive models and expectations of the cells on either side of the boundary.

As time goes by, due to the continuing sharing of experiences and learning, one of the remaining worldviews progressively gains ground over the other, until it alone survives. This is illustrated in Figure 17, which shows the same array evolution of Figure 16 but at a later period of time. *Here, the simulation clearly illustrates the power of shared experiences in driving an entire culture to give credit to a single worldview, even though reality itself is equally amenable to the idiosyncrasies of an arbitrary variety of worldviews.* Once this convergence to a single physics is complete, magic disappears from the world of manifestation. All cognitive models and expectations – that is, all state transition rules – are harmonized, consistent with one another and with the reality that actually manifests. At this point, the world of our metaphor becomes a world without mysteries; a world that, although entirely created and projected onto the fabric of space-time by the imaginations of its own inhabitants, behaves exactly as if

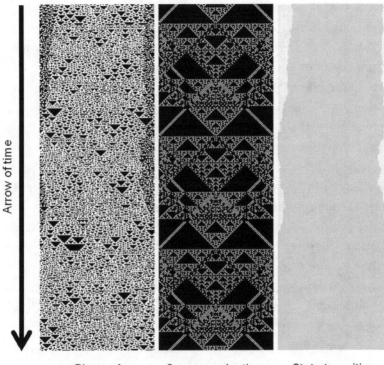

Plane of
manifestation

Source projection
plane

State transition
rules of the plane
of manifestation

Figure 17. A continuing overview of the further evolution of
states in the plane of manifestation (left) and in the Source
projection plane (center), as well as of the different state transition
rules operating in the plane of manifestation (right).

manifested reality were objective and independent of the individuals' participation in its making. Theirs becomes a world of science over dreams; of analysis over creativity. Their reality becomes, quite literally, *consensus reality*.

But that is not all. Remember that the different physics – that is, the different state transition rules – represented in the rightmost column of figures 16 and 17 encompass *both* what happens in the plane of manifestation *and* in the Source projection plane. The respective cell neighborhoods span both planes, as shown in Figure 15. The inhabitants of such world, instinctively as it may be, are still connected and attuned to the subtle cross-dimensional influences of the Source, as represented by the vertical dotted line in Figure 15. Theirs is still a world of intuition and sensitivity. The very recognition that a single and supreme "theory of everything" governs their world is dependent upon the acknowledgement of these cross-dimensional influences. Without such acknowledgement, their scientists would not be able to see the consistency of the behavior of nature, for essential variables would be missing. There would be an *appearance* of contradiction where harmony actually is pervasive. Indeed, if their expectations of reality were based purely on what they perceive in the plane of manifestation, manifested reality would actually contradict their now over-constrained cognitive models.

What would happen if the inhabitants of such a world at some point decided to ignore and even deny the cross-dimensional, fractal influences of the Source projection plane in their reality? How would they then see their world? What expectations would they project onto the fabric of space-time and what manifested reality would then emerge? One wonders if the simulations of our metaphor could enrich our thoughts on these questions. So let us try it out.

I adapted the simulation so that, at a certain point in the evolution of the plane of manifestation, *its cells simply stop looking at their counterparts in the Source projection plane.* In other words, I modified the neighborhood shown in Figure 15 by removing from it the light-grey cell in the Source projection plane. This way, each cell of the plane of manifestation now only acknowledges, looks at, or otherwise perceives its two neighbors in the plane of manifestation itself. In our metaphor, this represents a materialist denial of higher planes of reality and their influence in our lives; a "materialist paradigm," if you will. However, some influence from the Source remains: when the "vote" for determining a next cell state in the plane of manifestation is tied, it is *still* the corresponding cell state of the Source projection plane that makes the determination. So there is still influence from the Source exerted in the plane of manifestation. It operates as a kind of fractal bias – or tendency – in the underlying "quantum chance," which percolates up to manifestation when no unambiguous conscious choice is made. In the metaphor, the conscious entities represented by the cells of the plane of manifestation – ignoring, as they now do, the Source – would acknowledge this influence merely as the expression of quantum randomness, remaining unaware, due to the lack of a sufficient number of data samples, that it actually embodies a subtle but structured pattern in space-time.

Figure 18 illustrates the results of the corresponding simulations. Approximately half way from the top, the cells in the plane of manifestation stop taking into account the cross-dimensional inputs from the Source. Surprisingly, the triangular theme survives this transition and remains in the plane of manifestation, albeit with a twist: what had been black-filled triangles up until that point turns into white-filled triangles. *In a way, it is as though the very polarity of the plane of manifestation suddenly inverted.* Triangles that before were filled with live cells are now filled with dead cells. Yet the balanced combination between structure and chaos survives the transition to this "materialist paradigm" of cognition and beliefs. The resulting world remains

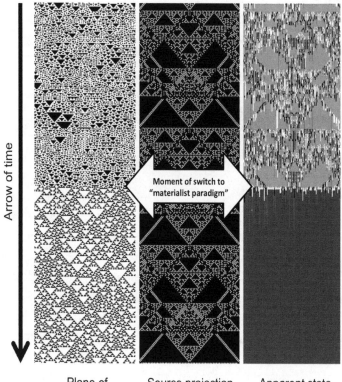

Arrow of time

Moment of switch to "materialist paradigm"

Plane of manifestation

Source projection plane

Apparent state transition rules of the plane of manifestation

Figure 18. An overview of the evolution of states in the plane of manifestation (left) and in the Source projection plane (center), as well as of the apparent state transition rules operating in the plane of manifestation (right), illustrating what happens at the moment a "materialist paradigm" is adopted.

one of novelty and meaning.

The explanation for this is as follows: although the cells of the plane of manifestation are no longer directly aware of the Source projection plane, they still learn – by adapting their respective state transition rules – from the states that actually manifest in their respective neighborhoods. Every time there is a tie in the conscious choice of a next cell state, that next cell state is then determined, as described earlier, by what happens in the Source projection plane. When the state so determined by the Source eventually manifests, the cells in the plane of manifestation learn that too. This way, their state transition rules end up learning and incorporating, indirectly and by bits and pieces, some of the fractal dynamics unfolding in the Source projection plane. In our metaphor, the conscious entities represented by the cells of the plane of manifestation are entirely unaware that their cognitive models are being indirectly influenced from another realm. They simply learn from what they see and then construct mental models that reflect their experiences. Eventually, through the sharing of experiences, they all converge to the exact same state transition rule. From this point on, there is never a tie in the conscious choice of a next cell state, for *all* cells are now projecting the same, consistent understanding of reality onto the fabric of space-time.

The rightmost column of Figure 18 now has a slightly different interpretation than in Figures 16 and 17. Instead of showing the spread of different state transition rules, it now illustrates the spread of *apparent* state transition rules, as construed from the point of view of an observer who ignores the existence of the Source projection plane. The apparent state transition rules are the rules implied by the observed state transitions when only the cells in the plane of manifestation are considered. In other words, they represent a pragmatic, *empirical* attempt to explain all state transitions *as if such transitions were caused solely by what happens in the plane of manifestation.* That is *not* how the automaton actually works before the switch to the materialist paradigm, but simply how an observer confined to the plane of manifestation would have tentatively *interpreted* it to work. Such an observer would ignore the causal influence of the Source, seeking *to empirically calibrate a model* of state transitions on the basis of observations of the plane of manifestation alone.

Before the transition to the materialist paradigm, one can see how dramatically such an explanatory approach would have failed to capture what is going on: multiple shades of grey are observed on the upper half of the rightmost column of Figure 18, indicating that many different and contradictory explanations of nature – or "theories of everything" – would be concurrently required. This variety of models would be necessary because certain causal elements of, or variables relevant to, what is going on are simply ignored. Therefore, the variability they entail must be captured in the structure of the explanation itself, leading to multiple and contradictory theories. Unsurprisingly, the variety of these "theories of everything" seems to increase along the main fractal contours of the unfolding Source projection pattern. *In a world attuned to the Source, scientists would certainly not fail to realize that the materialist paradigm would be an inappropriate explanation of manifested phenomena.*

However, from the moment the transition to the materialist paradigm takes place, things change very quickly. The *apparent* state transition rules now become equivalent to the *actual* state transition rules, since the cells of the plane of manifestation no longer take the Source projection plane into account in their respective neighborhoods. Notice that a single shade of grey takes over in the lower half of the rightmost column of Figure 18. This means that the cells very quickly adapt to the fact that the Source projection plane can no longer be perceived, coming up with an alternative worldview consistent with their now reduced cognitive abilities. There emerges a single "apparent" state transition rule representing *one* "theory of everything."

Although we have seen such convergence to a single physics happen before (see Figure 17), it is not obvious that it should happen again here. Indeed, this time the possible "theories of everything" have been arbitrarily constrained to the plane of manifestation, so their explanatory power is reduced. Yet, the materialist assumption alone – that is, the assumption that all experiences must be explainable purely by what happens in the plane of manifestation – allows a single, arbitrarily constrained "theory of everything" to still coherently explain all manifested phenomena and take over the entire culture. *The simulation dramatically illustrates the self-fulfilling power of the materialist assumption: merely by expecting manifested reality to be explainable by what can be seen in a now reduced perceptual field, the cells project a new version of manifested reality onto the fabric of space-time that indeed can be explained this way.* The simulation illustrates how learning in the context of shared experiences can easily lead to a manifested reality that behaves exactly as if it were objective and purely material, although such reality remains intrinsically subjective and hyper-dimensional. Materialist scientists in such a world would be able to claim, with overwhelming empirical confirmation, that their purely materialist models are sufficient to explain the manifested phenomena of nature in a causally-closed manner. Materialist science would triumph in this world, even though its success would be a mere artifact of people's choice to ignore subtle cross-dimensional inputs. The world these people live in, as an acquiescent mirror of their mental models and expectations, dutifully complies with the self-imposed limitations of their cognition.

Naturally, the idea that the entire population of the plane of manifestation would loose their intuitive connection with the Source is unreasonable. Unanimity is not an often observed phenomenon in our own world. Moreover, our simulations assume that cells in the plane of manifestation learn continuously and, other than the prejudice of ignoring the Source projection plane, without further biases. We know that is not how things normally work. Therefore, we could say that a more likely scenario, in the context of the metaphor, would be one where anomalies would remain: not all worldviews would be identical; not all manifestations would be consistent with the majority worldview. There would be cultural fringes in this more realistic metaphor. Some would claim to witness magic, psychic phenomena, fairies, UFOs, and the otherwise unexplainable. However, as our simulations suggest, these instances would likely be infrequent and ambiguous enough that they would not threaten the majority worldview.

Our metaphor, thus, has many-fold correspondences with the intuitions of subjective exploration, and even extends those intuitions beyond what we discussed in earlier chapters. It illustrates how a simple set of symmetric, elemental thought patterns in space-time (Figure 11) can produce, through recursion, an infinite unfolding of a composite, perfectly regular, fractal thought Pattern (Figures 12 and 13). It also shows that, if manifested reality is a lower-dimensional realm overlaid on a projection of the Source (Figure 15), then it is the cross-dimensional influence of the underlying Source that injects order and structure into the highly entropic and chaotic realm of manifestation. Indeed, it is through the subtle combination of *dis*order – generated by different conscious entities independently projecting their own individual expectations onto the fabric of manifested space-time – and order – injected cross-dimensionally into the realm of manifestation from the Source – that a structured but novelty-producing field of shared experience emerges (Figure 16). Moreover, through learning in the context of these shared experiences, those conscious entities tend to cluster and converge to common, shared worldviews, leading to the creation of a reality consistent with the assumption of objectivity (Figure 17). Finally, the metaphor informs us that an intentional choice to deny and ignore the causal role of the Source inverts the polarity of manifested reality but does not destroy the delicate balance between entropy and structure. In this polarity-inverted version of manifested reality, a purely materialist worldview correctly describes the phenomenality of manifested reality in a causally-closed manner (Figure 18), except perhaps for a few and far between anomalies.

Chapter 13

Closing thoughts

We have now come to the end of this journey; one with more questions than answers; more possibilities than solutions; more ideas than conclusions. Yet it is my hope that it has been a valid journey, for before one can focus one's gaze on a narrow set of possibilities about the nature of reality, one must first step back and look, open mindedly, at *all* possibilities, especially those that contradict one's own preconceptions, cultural biases, and prejudices. Finding out what *may* be true is, in a way, a more instructive and artistic endeavor than finding out what *is* true. The latter is elusive and slippery; the former abounds in riches. It is only the culture-induced stupor we live in that prevents us from raising our gaze and seeing the signs right in front of us. Have you ever paid close attention to where your thoughts wander during an after-lunch nap? Have you ever made an effort to consistently remember your weirdest dreams and associated impressions? Or the funny images and feelings that pop into your mind at night, in the dark, after perhaps a few days of camping on a quiet beach or mountain? Have you ever had a calm conversation with a schizophrenic, listening attentively to his or her views on reality while maintaining a sincerely non-patronizing attitude? Do you remember your own inner life as a young child? In all these things, dare I say, may lie hints to the possibilities of reality.

Ours is a curious culture. We discover an important and useful rule of thumb like Occam's Razor – the idea that the best explanation tends to be the one requiring the fewest new assumptions – and then extrapolate and abuse of it beyond the scope wherein it is reasonable. *Whoever said that nature operates according to the simplest mechanisms that we, mere primates with opposing thumbs, can make up with the three pounds of grey goo in our heads?* We discover an effective method for informing our efforts to leverage the materials and energies of nature – namely, the scientific method – and then elevate that utilitarian method to the level of supreme judge of the ontological truth. *Whoever said that what works is what is?* We eliminate mysteries merely by giving them names. We do not know what lies at the heart of matter, but we give it a few names – quarks, leptons, photons, gluons, mesons, etc. – and presto, we feel like it has all been explained. Do not get me wrong: the serious scientists that model and discover these things know full well the extent to which they do *not* know what is going on. But our psychology rewards us with a fuzzy warm feeling the moment we all start using the same name for something fundamentally not understood. Somehow, the magic of the mystery vanishes simply by the collective, almost ceremonial act of labeling it. This absurd mentality is so pervasive in our culture that we even teach our children by giving them the names of things instead of explanations. We tell them that objects fall because of "gravity." Fine, but what is gravity? How does it do what it does? Do *you* know?[1]

We seem to have collectively descended into a highly restrictive, cynical, disenchanted frame of mind. *We developed the worst and most pernicious of all illusions: the illusion of knowledge.* Of all unproductive fantasies, this is the worst in that it makes one believe that one can stop searching and questioning. How it happened that we came to this point, I do not pretend to know. I am not a historian, anthropologist, or psychologist. But that it *did* happen seems obvious to even a casual observation of our civilization. Yet we see some tentative reactions to this at the so-called fringes of our culture. We hear calls for the "re-unification" of science and spirituality in a kind of new-age-styled epistemological rebirth. My own view is that we must be exceedingly careful with our wishes here; for, if realized, they may leave us without both a working science and a fulfilling spirituality.

I believe the aspiration for a holistic view of reality is legitimate. But the integrative approach it entails does not need to deface the building blocks of the whole it seeks to build. Those building blocks may be complementary to one another the way they are. To construct a holistic worldview one does not need to rob science of the objectivity and skepticism that make it effective. Neither does one need to ground spirituality on matter – mysterious quantum matter as it may be. What one does need is to integrate the messages of both science and spirituality, open-mindedly but also critically, in a holistic but personal worldview that the individual him or herself is ultimately responsible for. What we need is to be thoughtful, critical, *honest with ourselves*, and to make up our own minds about what all the stories we hear might mean to us, whether these stories come from scientists, philosophers, mystics, clergymen, bloggers, the evening news anchor, or the bloke down the pub. A call for top-down cultural reform, legitimate as it may be, is no substitute for personal initiative and responsibility in determining one's own worldview. Ultimately, it all starts and ends with the individual.

This holistic worldview must, in my current opinion, be an *additional* tool of cognition that enriches our toolbox of models and methods without artificially pruning off existing options. It must be an *integration* of viewpoints at a higher level of understanding; a level where paradox, contradiction, and cognitive dissonance are *productive* steps towards greater insight. This holistic metaphysics does not require the defacement of the methods we already have, and which have proven useful. That said, *it does require – and this is a crucial point – that we look upon these methods with the correct perspective, for everything has its proper place and applicability*. Ontology transcends science, so to look to science for all ontological answers is misguided. Science just isn't the right tool for the job. Similarly, spirituality transcends matter, but when one appeals to spiritual forces to explain material phenomena for which more reasonable explanations exist, which better fit the evidence at hand, one may also be using the wrong tool for the job.

I am not suggesting here that we go back to the Cartesian divide between matter and spirit. No. My own personal philosophy is a monistic one – that is, one where all planes and aspects of existence are seen to be part of a unified whole. But it is, in my view, an observable fact that each of the methods we currently have at our disposal is, in isolation, insufficient to cover all potentially valid avenues of investigation. *The dualism I may be implying is thus not one of substance, but one of method.* Earlier, I highlighted how science starts from the premises that reality is objective and individual observation unreliable. A form of subjective exploration of nature that starts from the opposite premises – that is, that reality is subjective and our own individual observations are all we have – seems to me to be a necessary and complementary ingredient of any thorough and honest investigation of nature.

The value of subjective exploration for understanding reality may actually go beyond that of methodological completeness alone. As Carl Jung masterfully argued in his magnificent little book, "The Undiscovered Self,"[2] only the anchor of inner, transcendent experience can protect the individual from submersion into what he calls "mass-mindedness." Mass-mindedness, as embodied in the set of cultural values and reality models reigning in a society, replaces individual experience – *which is the only carrier of life and reality* – with conceptual averages. Jung went further to point at scientific education, when elevated to the position of ultimate ontological authority, as an enabler of mass-mindedness by imparting an unrealistic worldview based on statistical truths. This, he argued, blurs the patterns and nuances of reality into those –

ultimately unreal – conceptual averages.

The mysteries are thus many. If there is anything I can conclude with certainty from my own subjective explorations, it is this: *there is a lot more to reality than we think.* Whatever this uncharted territory may be – whether it is purely in the brain or exists outside of the brain – it is profoundly significant to one's own life and perspectives. It is the territory we, somehow, have come from but have since forgotten. An effort to chart this territory may entail a return to one's forgotten but true home and a re-acquaintance with one's forgotten but true self. As Jacques Vallée noted in closing his mesmerizing classic, "Passport to Magonia," "we cannot be sure that we study something real, because we do not know what reality is; we can only be sure that our study will help us understand more, far more, about ourselves."[3] I cannot think of greater adventure.

Appendix

Computer code

Here all the details of the computer algorithms used to generate Figures 12, 13, and 16 to 18 are shown. Initially, I thought of using symbolic mathematical notation to do this. However, ultimately I concluded that the computer code itself was a much less ambiguous, more direct and convenient alternative. Therefore, you will find below the code used to generate the figures.

The code has been written in "Processing," an open source programming language and environment, based on Java, with special support for animations. At the time this book was written, Processing and its extensive documentation could be freely downloaded from http://www.processing.org. If you intend to run the programs below yourself, you will need to have Processing installed in your system. In what follows, I will assume that anyone interested in the level of detail in this appendix is relatively at ease with programming languages like Java.

The first program, shown below, is the one used to create a metaphor for the "Source," as illustrated in Figures 12 and 13. It starts with some comments on how to use the program, as well as key variable declarations, which are also commented:

```
/* SOURCE METAPHOR
 *
 * USAGE:
 *    "l" to start and stop looping automatically over iterations;
 *    "s" to single-step to the next iteration, and then wait;
 *    "i" to re-initialize everything. */

int[][][] spaceTime; // Space-time fabric where Pattern unfolds
int[] ruleTable; // Array for storing state transition rule
```

```
int sx = 513; // X-dimension of space-time (power of 2, plus 1)
int sy = 513; // Y-dimension of space-time (power of 2, plus 1)
int counter = 0; // Counts number of iterations
int blockSize = 1; // Size, in pixels, of the side of a cell square
boolean stepMode = false; // Step-by-step or automatic looping
```

The next part of the code is the setup routine required by Processing. It defines the size of the window used to display the animation, the visual scheme used, and initializes some of the variables:

```
void setup() {
  size(sx * blockSize, sy * blockSize, P2D);
  colorMode(HSB, 1);
  background(1);
  noStroke();
  frameRate(24);
  spaceTime = new int[sx][sy][2];
  ruleTable = new int[] {0, 1, 1, 0, 1, 1, 1, 1, 1, 0, 1, 1};
  initialize();
  if (stepMode) {noLoop();}
}
```

The next segment is the drawing function required by Processing, responsible for the main animation loop:

```
void draw() {
  for (int x = 0; x < sx; x++) {
    for (int y = 0; y < sy; y++) {
      fill((spaceTime[x][y][0] == 0 ? 1:0));
      rect(x*blockSize, y*blockSize, blockSize, blockSize);
    }
  }
  println("Cycle: " + counter);
  if (stepMode) noLoop();
  counter++;
  update();
}
```

The function below is responsible for updating the states of the cellular automaton, carrying it over to the next generation:

```
void update() {
  for (int x = 0; x < sx; x++) {
    for (int y = 0; y < sy; y++) {
```

```
        spaceTime[x][y][1] = ruleTable[patternID(x, y)];
    }
  }
  for (int x = 0; x < sx; x++) {
    for (int y = 0; y < sy; y++) {
      spaceTime[x][y][0] = spaceTime[x][y][1];
    }
  }
}
```

To determine which of the twelve patterns illustrated in Figure 11 is present in a given neighborhood at a given iteration, it is convenient to, first, calculate the total number of live (black) cells in that neighborhood:

```
int neighborhoodTotal(int x, int y) {
  return spaceTime[x][y][0] +
         spaceTime[(x + 1) % sx][y][0] +
         spaceTime[x][(y + 1) % sy][0] +
         spaceTime[(x + sx - 1) % sx][y][0] +
         spaceTime[x][(y + sy - 1) % sy][0];
}
```

The function below can, then, actually identify which of those twelve patterns is at hand, using some computational shortcuts:

```
int patternID(int x, int y) {
  int result = 0;
  switch (neighborhoodTotal(x, y)) {
    case 0:
      result = 0;
      break;
    case 1:
      if (spaceTime[x][y][0] == 1) {result = 1;}
      else {result = 2;}
      break;
    case 2:
      if (spaceTime[x][y][0] == 1) {result = 3;}
      else {
        if (((spaceTime[(x + 1) % sx][y][0] == 1) &&
             (spaceTime[(x + sx - 1) % sx][y][0] == 1)) ||
            ((spaceTime[x][(y + 1) % sy][0] == 1) &&
             (spaceTime[x][(y + sy - 1) % sy][0] == 1)))
          {result = 5;}
        else {result = 4;}
      }
```

```
      break;
   case 3:
     if (spaceTime[x][y][0] == 0) {result = 7;}
     else {
       if (((spaceTime[(x + 1) % sx][y][0] == 1) &&
             (spaceTime[(x + sx - 1) % sx][y][0] == 1)) ||
            ((spaceTime[x][(y + 1) % sy][0] == 1) &&
             (spaceTime[x][(y + sy - 1) % sy][0] == 1)))
         {result = 8;}
       else {result = 6;}
     }
     break;
   case 4:
     if (spaceTime[x][y][0] == 1) {result = 9;}
     else {result = 10;}
     break;
   case 5:
     result = 11;
     break;
   }
   return result;
}
```

Here is some initialization code called early in the execution of the program. Notice that all cells are initialized to "dead" (white, or zero), while the center cell alone is initialized to "alive" (black, or one):

```
void initialize() {
  for (int x = 0; x < sx; x++) {
    for (int y = 0; y < sy; y++) {
      spaceTime[x][y][0] = 0;
    }
  }
  spaceTime[(sx-1)/2][(sy-1)/2][0] = 1;
  counter = 0;
}
```

Finally, the code responsible for reading the user's keyboard inputs to control the program:

```
void keyPressed() {
  if (key == 'i') {initialize();}
  if (key == 'l') {
    stepMode = !stepMode;
    if (!stepMode) loop();
```

```
  }
  if (key == 's') {
    if (!stepMode) {stepMode = true;}
    else {loop();}
  }
}
```

The code for generating Figure 14 can be derived trivially from the program above. Therefore, it will not be discussed here.

Now, below, you will find the complete code used to generate Figures 16 and 17. Keep in mind that this is an entirely separate, standalone program. Although the code for emulating the "Source" is repeated in it – since it is required for determining the "Source projection plane" – I will comment only on the new segments of the code, responsible for emulating the "plane of manifestation" and displaying the state transition rules with different shades of grey. Here is the beginning of the code where, once again, the variable declarations are commented so you can have an early idea about which variable represents what:

```
/* MANIFESTATION PLANE METAPHOR
 *
 * USAGE:
 *    "l" to start and stop looping automatically over iterations;
 *    "s" to single-step to the next iteration, and then wait;
 *    "i" to re-initialize everything. */

int[][] PlaneOfManifestation; // 1D plane of manifestation
int[][] PlaneOfManifestationFrame; // Corresponding image in time
int[][][] Source; // Arrays holding 2D Source
int[] SourceProjectionPlane; // 1D source projection plane
int[][] SourceProjectionPlaneFrame; // Corresponding image in time
int[][] ruleTable; // Random state transition rules
int[] RuleColor; // Color corresponding to a state transition rule
int[][] RuleColorFrame; // Corresponding image in time
int[][] learning; // Determines learned state transition rule
int[] SourceRule; // State transition rule of Source array
int blockSize = 2; // Size, in pixels, of side of cell square
int sx = 129; // X-dimension of Source array (power of 2, plus 1)
int sy = 129; // Y-dimension of Source array (power of 2, plus 1)
int row = (sy-1)/4; // Source row making up source projection plane
boolean stepMode = false; // Step-by-step or automatic looping
```

```
int cntr = 0; // Internal synchronization variable
```

The setup and drawing routines below are analogous to what we have discussed earlier, except that several new variables now need to be initialized, and then recursively updated within the main drawing loop:

```
void setup() {
    size(3*sx*blockSize + 10, 3*sy*blockSize, P2D);
    noStroke();
    colorMode(HSB, 32);
    background(#FFFFFF);
    frameRate(24);
    PlaneOfManifestation = new int[sx][2];
    PlaneOfManifestationFrame = new int[sx][3*sy];
    Source = new int[sx][sy][2];
    SourceProjectionPlane = new int[sx];
    SourceProjectionPlaneFrame = new int[sx][3*sy];
    ruleTable = new int[sx][5];
    RuleColor = new int[sx];
    RuleColorFrame = new int[sx][3*sy];
    SourceRule = new int[] {0, 1, 1, 0, 1, 1, 1, 1, 1, 0, 1, 1};
    learning = new int[sx][5];
    resetPlaneOfManifestation();
    resetSource();
    initializeRules();
}

void draw() {
    int total, count, ID;
    int result = 0;
    for (int x = 0; x < sx; x++) {
        PlaneOfManifestation[x][0] = PlaneOfManifestation[x][1];
    }
    for (int x = 0; x < sx; x++) {
        for (int y = 0; y < sy; y++) {
            Source[x][y][0] = Source[x][y][1];
        }
    }
    for (int x = 0; x < sx; x++) {
        SourceProjectionPlane[x] = Source[x][row][0];
    }
    for (int x = 0; x < sx; x++) {
        RuleColor[x] = ruleToNumber(x);
    }
    for (int x = 0; x < sx; x++) {
        for (int y = 0; y < (3*sy-1); y++) {
```

```
      PlaneOfManifestationFrame[x][y] =
         PlaneOfManifestationFrame[x][y+1];
      SourceProjectionPlaneFrame[x][y] =
         SourceProjectionPlaneFrame[x][y+1];
      RuleColorFrame[x][y] = RuleColorFrame[x][y+1];
   }
}
for (int x = 0; x < sx; x++) {
   PlaneOfManifestationFrame[x][3*sy-1] =
      PlaneOfManifestation[x][0];
   SourceProjectionPlaneFrame[x][3*sy-1] =
      SourceProjectionPlane[x];
   RuleColorFrame[x][3*sy-1] = RuleColor[x];
}
```

Here, the three columns of Figures 16 and 17 are actually drawn on the screen, after the corresponding variables have been updated above:

```
for (int x = 0; x < sx; x++) {
   for (int y = 0; y < 3*sy; y++) {
      if (PlaneOfManifestationFrame[x][y] == 1) {
         fill(#000000);
         rect(x*blockSize, y*blockSize, blockSize, blockSize);
      } else {
         fill(#FFFFFF);
         rect(x*blockSize, y*blockSize, blockSize, blockSize);
      }
      if (SourceProjectionPlaneFrame[x][y] == 1) {
         fill(#000000);
         rect((sx+x+5)*blockSize, y*blockSize, blockSize, blockSize);
      } else {
         fill(#FFFFFF);
         rect((sx+x+5)*blockSize, y*blockSize, blockSize, blockSize);
      }
      fill(RuleColorFrame[x][y]);
      rect((2*sx+x+10)*blockSize, y*blockSize, blockSize, blockSize);
   }
}
```

The next loop controls the transition of states in the 1D cellular automaton, corresponding to the "plane of manifestation," onto its next generation:

```
if (cntr > (((sy-1)/2)-row-2)) {
   for (int x = 0; x < sx; x++) {
```

In the lines below, the "vote" is performed across the three cells in a neighborhood within the plane of manifestation, to determine the next state of a cell. The cell's own vote counts twice those of its two neighbors in the plane of manifestation. Notice that, when a tie occurs, the next state is determined directly by the Source projection plane:

```
ID = neighborhoodTotal(x);
total = ruleTable[(x + sx - 1) % sx][ID] +
          2*ruleTable[x][ID] +
          ruleTable[(x + 1) % sx][ID];
switch (total) {
  case 4: PlaneOfManifestation[x][1] = 1; break;
  case 3: PlaneOfManifestation[x][1] = 1; break;
  case 2: PlaneOfManifestation[x][1] =
            SourceProjectionPlane[x]; break;
  case 1: PlaneOfManifestation[x][1] = 0; break;
  case 0: PlaneOfManifestation[x][1] = 0; break;
}
```

Now, the cells must learn from the states that actually "manifest" after the vote. They learn not only from "direct experience," but also from experiences "communicated" from their two neighbors in the plane of manifestation. Notice that learning from direct experience is twice as strong as learning from what is communicated from neighbors:

```
if (PlaneOfManifestation[x][1] == 1) {
  learning[(x + sx - 1) % sx][ID]++;
  learning[x][ID] += 2;
  learning[(x + 1) % sx][ID]++;
} else {
  learning[(x + sx - 1) % sx][ID]--;
  learning[x][ID] -= 2;
  learning[(x + 1) % sx][ID]--;
}
}
transferLearning();
} else {cntr++;}
```

Now the Source is updated to its next generation:

```
  for (int x = 0; x < sx; x++) {
    for (int y = 0; y < sy; y++) {
      Source[x][y][1] = SourceRule[patternID(x, y)];
    }
  }
  if (stepMode) noLoop();
}
```

In the lines that follow, the resulting learning of the cells is transferred to their respective state transition rules, so the next generation of the automaton representing the plane of manifestation will be determined by these new, learned rules.

```
void transferLearning() {
  for (int x = 0; x < sx; x++) {
    for (int r = 0; r < 5; r++) {
      if (learning[x][r] > 0) {
        ruleTable[x][r] = 1;
      }
      if (learning[x][r] < 0) {
        ruleTable[x][r] = 0;
      }
      learning[x][r] = 0;
    }
  }
}
```

Below, the total amount of "live" cells in the cross-dimensional neighborhood shown in Figure 15 is counted, for the cellular automaton representing the plane of manifestation is a "totalistic cellular automaton;" that is, one that only considers the total amount of live cells in a neighborhood, not their specific configuration. This is done to simplify the metaphor and make its interpretation easier.

```
int neighborhoodTotal(int x) {
  return PlaneOfManifestation[(x + sx - 1) % sx][0] +
         PlaneOfManifestation[x][0] +
         PlaneOfManifestation[(x + 1) % sx][0] +
         SourceProjectionPlane[x];
}
```

The routine below is used to convert a specific state transition rule into a single, unique number, so it can then be used to determine the shade of gray that is displayed in the rightmost column of Figures 16 and 17:

```
int ruleToNumber(int x) {
  String ID = str(ruleTable[x][1]);
  for (int i = 1; i < 4; i++) {
    ID += str(ruleTable[x][i]);
  }
  return(unbinary(ID));
}
```

Now we have some reset and initialization functions to refresh the arrays. Notice that the plane of manifestation starts with a single "live" (black) cell in its center. Notice also that the state transition rule of each cell in the plane of manifestation is randomly, and independently, initialized:

```
void resetPlaneOfManifestation() {
  for (int x = 0; x < sx; x++) {
    PlaneOfManifestation[x][1] = 0;
  }
  PlaneOfManifestation[(sx-1)/2][1] = 1;
}

void resetSource() {
  for (int x = 0; x < sx; x++) {
    for (int y = 0; y < sy; y++) {
      Source[x][y][1] = 0;
    }
  }
  Source[(sx-1)/2][(sy-1)/2][1] = 1;
}

void initializeRules() {
  for (int x = 0; x < sx; x++) {
    ruleTable[x][0] = 0; // Quiescent state 0
    for (int r = 1; r < 4; r++) {
      ruleTable[x][r] = round(random(1));
    }
    ruleTable[x][4] = 1; // Quiescent state 1
  }
```

```
        resetPlaneOfManifestation();
}
```

The remaining code controls the unfolding of the Source Pattern, used to determine the contents of the "Source projection plane," as already discussed earlier:

```
int vonneummanNeighborhood(int x, int y) {
    return Source[x][y][0] +
           Source[(x + 1) % sx][y][0] +
           Source[x][(y + 1) % sy][0] +
           Source[(x + sx - 1) % sx][y][0] +
           Source[x][(y + sy - 1) % sy][0];
}

int patternID(int x, int y) {
    int result = 0;
    switch (vonneummanNeighborhood(x, y)) {
      case 0:
        result = 0;
        break;
      case 1:
        if (Source[x][y][0] == 1) {result = 1;}
        else {result = 2;}
        break;
      case 2:
        if (Source[x][y][0] == 1) {result = 3;}
        else {
          if (((Source[(x + 1) % sx][y][0] == 1) &&
                (Source[(x + sx - 1) % sx][y][0] == 1)) ||
               ((Source[x][(y + 1) % sy][0] == 1) &&
                (Source[x][(y + sy - 1) % sy][0] == 1)))
            {result = 5;}
          else {result = 4;}
        }
        break;
      case 3:
        if (Source[x][y][0] == 0) {result = 7;}
        else {
          if (((Source[(x + 1) % sx][y][0] == 1) &&
                (Source[(x + sx - 1) % sx][y][0] == 1)) ||
               ((Source[x][(y + 1) % sy][0] == 1) &&
                (Source[x][(y + sy - 1) % sy][0] == 1)))
            {result = 8;}
          else {result = 6;}
        }
        break;
      case 4:
```

```
      if (Source[x][y][0] == 1) {result = 9;}
      else {result = 10;}
      break;
    case 5:
      result = 11;
      break;
    }
  return result;
}
```

Finally, the minimalistic user interface code:

```
void keyPressed() {
  if (key == 'i') {
    initializeRules();
    resetPlaneOfManifestation();
    resetSource();
    cntr = 0;
  }
  if (key == 'l') {
    stepMode = !stepMode;
    if (!stepMode) loop();
  }
  if (key == 's') {
    if (!stepMode) {stepMode = true;}
    else {loop();}
  }
}
```

The third and last program, used to generate Figure 18, is shown below. It is very similar to the program already discussed above, so I will comment only on the segments that are different. Notice that, at some point, the user must push the space bar in order to trigger the transition to the "materialistic paradigm."

```
/* MATERIALISTIC PARADIGM METAPHOR
 *
 * USAGE:
 *    "l" to start and stop looping automatically over iterations;
 *    "s" to single-step to the next iteration, and then wait;
 *    "i" to re-initialize everything.
 *    " " to switch to materialistic paradigm, and back */

int[][] PlaneOfManifestation; // 1D plane of manifestation
int[][] PlaneOfManifestationFrame; // Corresponding image in time
```

```
int[][][] Source; // Arrays holding 2D Source
int[] SourceProjectionPlane; // 1D source projection plane
int[][] SourceProjectionPlaneFrame; // Corresponding image in time
int[][] ruleTable; // State transition rules
int[] RuleColor; // Color corresp. to apparent state transition rule
int[][] RuleColorFrame; // Corresponding image in time
int[][] learning; // Determines learned state transition rule
int[] SourceRule; // State transition rule of Source array
int[][] empiricalRule; // Apparent state transition rules
int blockSize = 2; // Size, in pixels, of side of cell square
int sx = 129; // X-dimension of Source array (power of 2, plus 1)
int sy = 129; // Y-dimension of Source array (power of 2, plus 1)
int row = (sy-1)/4; // Source row making up source projection plane
boolean stepMode = false; // Step-by-step or automatic looping
boolean materialistic = false; // Materialistic paradigm active?
int cntr = 0; // Internal synchronization variable

void setup() {
  size(3*sx*blockSize + 10, 3*sy*blockSize, P2D);
  noStroke();
  colorMode(HSB, 16);
  background(#FFFFFF);
  frameRate(24);
  PlaneOfManifestation = new int[sx][2];
  PlaneOfManifestationFrame = new int[sx][3*sy];
  Source = new int[sx][sy][2];
  SourceProjectionPlane = new int[sx];
  SourceProjectionPlaneFrame = new int[sx][3*sy];
  ruleTable = new int[sx][5];
  RuleColor = new int[sx];
  RuleColorFrame = new int[sx][3*sy];
  SourceRule = new int[] {0, 1, 1, 0, 1, 1, 1, 1, 1, 0, 1, 1};
  learning = new int[sx][5];
  empiricalRule = new int[sx][4];
  resetPlaneOfManifestation();
  resetSource();
  initializeRules();
}

void draw()  {
  int total, count, ID;
  int result = 0;
  for (int x = 0; x < sx; x++) {
    updateEmpiricalRule(x);
  }
  for (int x = 0; x < sx; x++) {
    RuleColor[x] = ruleToNumber(x);
  }
  for (int x = 0; x < sx; x++) {
    PlaneOfManifestation[x][0] = PlaneOfManifestation[x][1];
  }
```

175

```
for (int x = 0; x < sx; x++) {
  for (int y = 0; y < sy; y++) {
    Source[x][y][0] = Source[x][y][1];
  }
}
for (int x = 0; x < sx; x++) {
  SourceProjectionPlane[x] = Source[x][row][0];
}
for (int x = 0; x < sx; x++) {
  for (int y = 0; y < (3*sy-1); y++) {
    PlaneOfManifestationFrame[x][y] =
      PlaneOfManifestationFrame[x][y+1];
    SourceProjectionPlaneFrame[x][y] =
      SourceProjectionPlaneFrame[x][y+1];
    RuleColorFrame[x][y] = RuleColorFrame[x][y+1];
  }
}
for (int x = 0; x < sx; x++) {
  PlaneOfManifestationFrame[x][3*sy-1] = PlaneOfManifestation[x][0];
  SourceProjectionPlaneFrame[x][3*sy-1] = SourceProjectionPlane[x];
  RuleColorFrame[x][3*sy-1] = RuleColor[x];
}
for (int x = 0; x < sx; x++) {
  for (int y = 0; y < 3*sy; y++) {
    if (PlaneOfManifestationFrame[x][y] == 1) {
      fill(#000000);
      rect(x*blockSize, y*blockSize, blockSize, blockSize);
    } else {
      fill(#FFFFFF);
      rect(x*blockSize, y*blockSize, blockSize, blockSize);
    }
    if (SourceProjectionPlaneFrame[x][y] == 1) {
      fill(#000000);
      rect((sx+x+5)*blockSize, y*blockSize, blockSize, blockSize);
    } else {
      fill(#FFFFFF);
      rect((sx+x+5)*blockSize, y*blockSize, blockSize, blockSize);
    }
    fill(RuleColorFrame[x][y]);
    rect((2*sx+x+10)*blockSize, y*blockSize, blockSize, blockSize);
  }
}
if (cntr > (((sy-1)/2)-row-2)) {
  for (int x = 0; x < sx; x++) {
    ID = neighborhoodTotal(x);
    total = ruleTable[(x + sx - 1) % sx][ID] +
            2*ruleTable[x][ID] +
            ruleTable[(x + 1) % sx][ID];
    switch (total) {
      case 4: PlaneOfManifestation[x][1] = 1; break;
      case 3: PlaneOfManifestation[x][1] = 1; break;
```

```
    case 2: PlaneOfManifestation[x][1] =
              SourceProjectionPlane[x]; break;
    case 1: PlaneOfManifestation[x][1] = 0; break;
    case 0: PlaneOfManifestation[x][1] = 0; break;
    }
    if (PlaneOfManifestation[x][1] == 1) {
      learning[(x + sx - 1) % sx][ID]++;
      learning[x][ID] += 2;
      learning[(x + 1) % sx][ID]++;
    } else {
      learning[(x + sx - 1) % sx][ID]--;
      learning[x][ID] -= 2;
      learning[(x + 1) % sx][ID]--;
    }
  }
  transferLearning();
  } else {cntr++;}
  for (int x = 0; x < sx; x++) {
    for (int y = 0; y < sy; y++) {
      Source[x][y][1] = SourceRule[patternID(x, y)];
    }
  }
  if (stepMode) noLoop();
}

void transferLearning() {
  for (int x = 0; x < sx; x++) {
    for (int r = 0; r < 5; r++) {
      if (learning[x][r] > 0) {
        ruleTable[x][r] = 1;
      }
      if (learning[x][r] < 0) {
        ruleTable[x][r] = 0;
      }
      learning[x][r] = 0;
    }
  }
}
```

In the function below, the state of the cell in the Source projection plane is only added, in calculating the corresponding neighborhood total, if the "materialistic paradigm" is *not* active. Otherwise, it is ignored, in a metaphor for the fact that the cells in the plane of manifestation no longer perceive the cross-dimensional influences from the Source.

```
int neighborhoodTotal(int x) {
  int total;
```

```
total = PlaneOfManifestation[(x + sx - 1) % sx][0] +
        PlaneOfManifestation[x][0] +
        PlaneOfManifestation[(x + 1) % sx][0];
if (!materialistic) {
   total += SourceProjectionPlane[x];
}
return total;
}
```

The function below tracks the "apparent" state transition rules used in the plane of manifestation; that is, it represents an empirical model of the phenomena and circumstances observed in the plane of manifestation alone. Remember that the cellular automaton used is a totalistic one, so only the total number of "live" cells matters.

```
void updateEmpiricalRule(int x) {
   int total = PlaneOfManifestation[(x + sx - 1) % sx][0] +
               PlaneOfManifestation[x][0] +
               PlaneOfManifestation[(x + 1) % sx][0];
   empiricalRule[x][total] = PlaneOfManifestation[x][1];
}
```

In the routine immediately below, each "apparent" state transition rule is converted into a unique number, representing a shade of gray, which is then displayed in the rightmost column of Figure 18.

```
int ruleToNumber(int x) {
   String ID = str(empiricalRule[x][0]);
   for (int i = 1; i < 4; i++) {
      ID += str(empiricalRule[x][i]);
   }
   return(unbinary(ID));
}

void resetPlaneOfManifestation() {
   for (int x = 0; x < sx; x++) {
      PlaneOfManifestation[x][1] = round(random(1));
   }
}

void resetSource() {
   for (int x = 0; x < sx; x++) {
```

```
    for (int y = 0; y < sy; y++) {
      Source[x][y][1] = 0;
    }
  }
  Source[(sx-1)/2][(sy-1)/2][1] = 1;
}
```

Unlike the previous program, this time the state transition rule of each cell in the plane of manifestation is initialized in the same way. This can be seen in the function immediately below. The idea is that we are no longer interested in the emergence of a single rule from a variety of randomly initialized ones, but solely in what happens at the moment of transition to a "materialistic paradigm" once the system has already converged to a uniform worldview.

```
void initializeRules() {
  for (int x = 0; x < sx; x++) {
    ruleTable[x][0] = 0;
    ruleTable[x][1] = 1;
    ruleTable[x][2] = 0;
    ruleTable[x][3] = 0;
    ruleTable[x][4] = 1;
  }
  resetPlaneOfManifestation();
}

int vonneummanNeighborhood(int x, int y) {
  return Source[x][y][0] +
         Source[(x + 1) % sx][y][0] +
         Source[x][(y + 1) % sy][0] +
         Source[(x + sx - 1) % sx][y][0] +
         Source[x][(y + sy - 1) % sy][0];
}

int patternID(int x, int y) {
  int result = 0;
  switch (vonneummanNeighborhood(x, y)) {
    case 0:
      result = 0;
      break;
    case 1:
      if (Source[x][y][0] == 1) {result = 1;}
      else {result = 2;}
      break;
    case 2:
```

```
      if (Source[x][y][0] == 1) {result = 3;}
      else {
        if (((Source[(x + 1) % sx][y][0] == 1) &&
             (Source[(x + sx - 1) % sx][y][0] == 1)) ||
            ((Source[x][(y + 1) % sy][0] == 1) &&
             (Source[x][(y + sy - 1) % sy][0] == 1)))
          {result = 5;}
        else {result = 4;}
      }
      break;
    case 3:
      if (Source[x][y][0] == 0) {result = 7;}
      else {
        if (((Source[(x + 1) % sx][y][0] == 1) &&
             (Source[(x + sx - 1) % sx][y][0] == 1)) ||
            ((Source[x][(y + 1) % sy][0] == 1) &&
             (Source[x][(y + sy - 1) % sy][0] == 1)))
          {result = 8;}
        else {result = 6;}
      }
      break;
    case 4:
      if (Source[x][y][0] == 1) {result = 9;}
      else {result = 10;}
      break;
    case 5:
      result = 11;
      break;
    }
  return result;
}


void keyPressed() {
  if (key == 'i') {
    initializeRules();
    resetPlaneOfManifestation();
    resetSource();
    cntr = 0;
  }
  if (key == 'l') {
    stepMode = !stepMode;
    if (!stepMode) loop();
  }
  if (key == 's') {
    if (!stepMode) {stepMode = true;}
    else {loop();}
  }
  if (key == ' ') {materialistic = !materialistic;}
}
```

Endnotes

Chapter 1

1   Jostein Gaarder, "Sophie's World: A Novel about the History of Philosophy," Berkley, 1996.

2   Throughout this book, I consistently use the qualifier "emergent" in its systems theory context. This way, something is said to be "emergent" when it consists of a new property or behavior of a system not directly traceable to the system's components, but rather to how those components interact. The emergent property is thus not a property of any component of the system, but only of the system as a whole. There is no central "command" that instructs a system to generate or display an emergent property; instead, it arises "spontaneously" out of the non-centralized, distributed interactions among the system's constituent elements. Examples of emergent phenomena are, for instance: complex ripple patterns in sand dunes; the architectural structure of termite mounds; the pattern of network paths in the Internet; etc. An excellent selection of papers on emergent phenomena and their implications to science and philosophy can be found here: Mark A. Bedau and Paul Humphreys (editors), "Emergence: Contemporary Readings in Philosophy and Science," MIT Press, May 2008.

Chapter 2

1   Terence McKenna, "True Hallucinations: being an account of the author's extraordinary adventures in the devil's paradise," HarperSanFrancisco, 1993, p. 203.

2   See, for instance: Maximilian Schlosshauer, "Decoherence, the measurement problem, and interpretations of quantum mechanics," Reviews of Modern Physics, Vol. 76(4), doi:10.1103/RevModPhys.76.1267, 2005, pp. 1267-1305.

3   During the Second World War, the American military used isolated pacific islands as bases and supply hubs. The native inhabitants of these islands, having had never seen technology before, were in awe of the aircraft and supplies suddenly pouring into their backyards. For their help, they were awarded food items and other modern "cargo." To the natives, the Americans were Gods magically descended from the skies bearing gifts. After the war, with the departure of the Americans, the natives created entire religious cults around their experiences. Mock airstrips, control towers, and even aircraft imitations were constructed and used in rituals aimed at invoking the return of the "Gods" and their "cargo." Though the natives could imitate the *form* of the airstrips and aircraft, naturally that was not enough to replicate the *function* and ultimate *result* of the real thing – namely, the delivery of real cargo. See Feynman's original "cargo cult" metaphor in: Richard P. Feynman, "The Pleasure of Finding Things Out," Perseus Publishing, 1999, pp. 208-209.

4   These considerations are reminiscent of solipsism, a skeptical hypothesis in philosophy that postulates that one's own mind is all that one can be sure to exist. After all, everything we believe to perceive, including other people and what they do or say, are only objects in our own minds. The most extreme derivation of solipsism is that you live your entire life in a kind of "matrix" of your own mind, and that nothing else exists. See, for instance: Stephen P. Thornton, "Solipsism and the Problem of Other Minds," Internet Encyclopedia of Philosophy, 24 October 2004.

5   Robert Lanza, "A New Theory of the Universe: Biocentrism builds on quantum physics by putting life into the equation," TheAmericanScholar.org, spring 2007.

6   Ray Tallis, "You won't find consciousness in the brain," NewScientist 2742, 7 January 2010.

Chapter 3

1   See: Mark F. X. Lythgoe *et al.*, "Obsessive, prolific artistic output following subarachnoid haemorrhage," Neurology, Vol. 64, 2005, pp. 397-398.
2   "What Makes a Genius?" BBC Horizon, Season 2009-2010.
3   Aldous Huxley, "The Doors of Perception and Heaven and Hell," Vintage Books, London, 2004.
4   Bernardo Kastrup, "Rationalist Spirituality: An exploration of the meaning of life and existence informed by logic and science," O Books, 2011.
5   See, for instance: Jeffrey M. Schwartz, Henry P. Stapp, and Mario Beauregard, "Quantum physics in neuroscience and psychology: a neurophysical model of mind–brain interaction," Philosophical Transactions of the Royal Society B, doi:10.1098/rstb.2004.1598, 2005.
6   See, for instance: Roger Penrose, Abner Shimony, Nancy Cartwright, and Stephen Hawking, "The Large, the Small, and the Human Mind," Cambridge University Press, 1997.
7   Ervin László, "Science and the Akashic Field: An Integral Theory of Everything," Inner Traditions, 2nd edition, May 2007.
8   See, for instance: David J. Chalmers, "Facing Up to the Problem of Consciousness," Journal of Consciousness Studies, Vol. 2(3), 1995, pp. 200-219.
9   David J. Chalmers, "The Puzzle of Conscious Experience," Scientific American, Vol. 12(1), Special Edition "The Hidden Mind," 2002, p. 96.

Chapter 4

1   See, for instance: Peter Russell, "The TM Technique," Peter Russell, November 2002.
2   John Hagelin, "Is consciousness the unified field? A field theorist's perspective," Modern Science and Vedic Science, Vol. 1, 1987, pp. 29-87.

3 David H. Freedman, "The new theory of everything," Discover, 1991, pp. 54–61.

4 Alberto Perez-De-Albeniz and Jeremy Holmes, "Meditation: concepts, effects and uses in therapy," International Journal of Psychotherapy, Vol. 5(1), doi:10.1080/13569080050020263, March 2000, pp. 49–59.

5 Raymond Bernard, "Messages from the Celestial Sanctum," AMORC, March 1980.

6 The idea that dreams provide a window into the collective unconscious has been discussed, for instance, in: Carl G. Jung (Author) and Anthony Storr (Editor), "The Essential Jung," Princeton University Press, December 1999.

7 Carl G. Jung, "The archetypes and the collective unconscious," Princeton University Press, 1980, p. 43.

8 D. M. Wegner, R. M. Wenzlaff, and M. Kozak, "The Return of Suppressed Thoughts in Dreams," Psychological Science, Vol. 15(4), doi:10.1111/j.0963-7214.2004.00657.x., 2004, p. 235.

9 Tsuneo Watanabe, "Lucid Dreaming: Its Experimental Proof and Psychological Conditions," Journal of International Society of Life Information Science (Japan), Vol. 21(1), March 2003, pp. 159–162.

10 Stephen LaBerge, "Exploring the World of Lucid Dreaming," Ballantine Books, November 1991.

11 See, for instance: C. Smith et al., "A randomised comparative trial of yoga and relaxation to reduce stress and anxiety," Complementary Therapies in Medicine, Vol. 15(2), June 2007, pp. 77-83.

12 See, for instance: David Siever, "Audio-visual entrainment: history, physiology, and clinical studies," appearing in: James R. Evans (editor), "Handbook of Neurofeedback: Dynamics and Clinical Applications," The Haworth Press Inc., September 2006, pp. 155-183.

13 See, for instance: Joseph Glicksohn, "Photic Driving and Altered States of Consciousness: An Exploratory Study,"

Imagination, Cognition and Personality, Vol. 6(2), 1986-1987, pp. 167-182.

14   See, for instance: Jiří Wackermann, Peter Pütz, and Carsten Allefeld, "Ganzfeld-induced hallucinatory experience, its phenomenology and cerebral electrophysiology," Cortex, Vol. 44(10), November-December 2008, pp. 1364-1378.

15   See, for instance: John Palmer, "ESP in the Ganzfeld: Analysis of a Debate," Journal of Consciousness Studies, Vol. 10(6-7), 2003, pp. 51-68.

16   See, for instance: Graham F. A. Harding and Peter M. Jeavons, "Photosensitive Epilepsy," Mac Keith Press, January 1994.

17   Michael Winkelman and Thomas B. Roberts, "Psychedelic Medicine: New evidence for hallucinogenic substances as treatments," Volumes 1 and 2, Praeger, June 2007.

18   See, for instance: Kenneth R. Alper, et al., "Treatment of Acute Opioid Withdrawal with Ibogaine," American Journal on Addictions, Vol. 8(3), doi:10.1080/105504999305848, 1999, pp. 234-242; as well as: Michael Winkelman and Thomas B. Roberts, op. cit., 2007, Volume 2, Section 1, "Treating Substance Abuse."

19   Terence McKenna, "The Archaic Revival," HarperOne, 1992, p. 27.

20   Terence McKenna, op. cit., 1992, p. 36.

21   Rick Strassman, "DMT: The Spirit Molecule," Park Street Press, 2001, p. 266.

22   Rick Strassman, op. cit., 2001, p. 310.

23   Rick Strassman et al., "Inner Paths to Outer Space," Park Street Press, 2008, pp. 268-298.

24   R. R. Griffiths et al., "Psilocybin can occasion mystical-type experiences having substantial and sustained personal meaning and spiritual significance," Psychopharmacology, Vol. 187, doi:10.1007/s00213-006-0457-5, 2006, p. 279.

25   It should be noted that I take no responsibility – legal,

medical, psychological, spiritual, or otherwise – for any problem or difficulty that anyone may face as a result of manufacturing, possessing, distributing, or using an entheogen, or any psychoactive substance for that matter.

26 See, for instance: Kylea Taylor, "The Breathwork Experience: Exploration and Healing in Nonordinary States of Consciousness," Hanford Mead Publishers, October 1994.

27 Joseph P. Rhinewine and Oliver J. Williams, "Holotropic Breathwork: The Potential Role of a Prolonged, Voluntary Hyperventilation Procedure as an Adjunct to Psychotherapy," The Journal of Alternative and Complementary Medicine, Vol. 13(7), doi:10.1089/acm.2006 .6203, September 2007, p. 775.

28 See, for instance: Yulia Ustinova, "Caves and the Ancient Greek Mind: Descending Underground in the Search for Ultimate Truth," Oxford University Press, April 2009.

29 See, for instance: Dennis R. Wier, "Trance: From Magic to Technology," Transmedia, May 1996.

Chapter 6
1 Carl G. Jung, "Psychology and Alchemy," Second Edition, Routledge, 1968, p. 99.

Chapter 8
1 For a functional description of how this may happen in the brain, see: Jeffrey M. Schwartz, Henry P. Stapp, and Mario Beauregard, *op. cit.*, 2005.

2 I am not implying that such principle is deterministic. Therefore, I am not implying that reality is deterministic. In fact, what I registered from the experience is the notion that such principle governs the unraveling of a primordial and free-willed imagination into its multiple underlying polarities, so variety is generated from unity. This way, if reality resides in a free-willed imagination, then reality is neces-

sarily not deterministic.

3   A good reference on fractals is: Kenneth Falconer, "Fractal Geometry: Mathematical Foundations and Applications," Wiley-Blackwell, 2nd Edition, September 2003.

Chapter 10

1   Notice that *direct* perception by consciousness is, in itself, nothing farfetched. After all, consciousness has direct perception of some of the electrochemical signals circulating in the brain.

2   I can imagine that elemental thought patterns could be cognized in different ways by different individuals. In my case, I cognized them visually, as geometric forms. Others could perhaps cognize them as musical tones and harmonies, or even as emotional archetypes.

3   The Ouroboros is the mythical serpent (or dragon) that swallows its own tail, forming a circle. It is an ancient symbol of cyclicality and self-reference.

Chapter 11

1   Simon Gröblacher *et al.*, "An experimental test of non-local realism," Nature 446, doi:10.1038/nature05677, 19 April 2007, pp. 871-875.

2   I elaborate much more extensively on this in my previous work, "Rationalist Spirituality," cited earlier (Bernardo Kastrup, *op. cit.*, 2011).

3   For a beautiful and modern articulation of the ideas behind Sacred Geometry, see: John Mitchell, "How the World is Made: The Story of Creation According to Sacred Geometry," Thames & Hudson, 2009.

4   Ian Stewart, "Why Beauty Is Truth: A History of Symmetry," Basic Books, 2007.

5   A. Garret Lisi, "An Exceptionally Simple Theory of Everything," arXiv:0711.0770v1 [hep-th], 6 November 2007.

[6]   See A. Garret Lisi, *op. cit.*, 2007, Figures 2, 3, and 4.

[7]   See Garrett Lisi's talk at TED2008, titled "Garrett Lisi on his theory of everything," February 2008.

[8]   See, for instance: Brian Greene, "The Elegant Universe: Superstrings, Hidden Dimensions and the Quest for the Ultimate Theory," Vintage, February 2000.

[9]   Benoit B. Mandelbrot, "The Fractal Geometry of Nature," W. H. Freeman, 1983.

[10]   Simon Gröblacher *et al.*, *op. cit.*, 2007, p. 871.

[11]   Rupert Sheldrake, Terence McKenna, and Ralph Abraham, "The Evolutionary Mind: Conversations on Science, Imagination & Spirit," Monkfish Book Publishing Company, 2005, pp. 166-168.

[12]   The placebo effect can go way beyond mere psychological benefits from swallowing sugar pills. This has been dramatically illustrated, for instance, in an extraordinary clinical trial carried out in 2002: patients who, instead of a real arthroscopy of the knee, got a fake – that is, placebo – surgery for osteoarthritis displayed the same long-term improvements as patients who were subjected to the real surgery. For more details, see: J. Bruce Moseley *et al.*, "A Controlled Trial of Arthroscopic Surgery for Osteoarthritis of the Knee," The New England Journal of Medicine, Vol. 347, 11 July 2002, pp. 81-88.

[13]   See, for instance: Steve Silberman, "Placebos Are Getting More Effective. Drugmakers Are Desperate to Know Why," Wired magazine, Issue 17.09, 24 August 2009.

[14]   Rupert Sheldrake quoted in: Rupert Sheldrake, Terence McKenna, and Ralph Abraham, *op. cit.*, 2005, pp. 167-168.

[15]   See, for instance: Stephen H. Kellert, "In the Wake of Chaos: Unpredictable Order in Dynamical Systems," University Of Chicago Press, 1993; particularly pp. 10-20.

[16]   See, for instance: Seth Lloyd, "Programming the Universe: A Quantum Computer Scientist Takes on the Cosmos," Alfred

A. Knopf, 2006; particularly pp. 48-50.

[17]   Seth Lloyd, *op. cit.*, 2006, p. 50.

[18]   Rupert Sheldrake, Terence McKenna, and Ralph Abraham, "Chaos, Creativity, and Cosmic Consciousness," Park Street Press, 2001, pp. 41-44.

Chapter 12

[1]   Ralph Abraham, quoted in: Rupert Sheldrake, Terence McKenna, and Ralph Abraham, *op. cit.*, 2005, p. 29.

[2]   See, for instance: Andrew Ilachinski, "Cellular Automata: A Discrete Universe," World Scientific, July 2001.

[3]   In his 1969 book *"Rechnender Raum"* ("calculating space"), Konrad Zuse postulated that the universe is being computed in real-time in a cellular-automaton-like substrate. Zuse's was the first book in the field of "digital physics," whose basic premise is that reality is essentially informational and, therefore, computable. The work of Seth Lloyd mentioned above (Seth Lloyd, *op. cit.*, 2006) essentially proposes a modern, quantum articulation of digital physics. In a way, an implication of these and other related works is that reality is the output of a kind of simulation.

[4]   See, for instance: Bastien Chopard and Michel Droz, "Cellular Automata Modeling of Physical Systems," Cambridge University Press, June 2005.

[5]   See, for instance: Mitchell Whitelaw, "Metacreation: Art and Artificial Life," The MIT Press, March 2004; particularly Chapter 5, "Abstract Machines."

[6]   Synchronicity is a kind of meaningful, yet unlikely, coincidence. First described by Carl Jung, the unlikely correlation between synchronistic events is perceived to be very meaningful by the person who experiences them, although the events themselves appear to be causally unrelated – that is, they cannot be said to either cause one another or to both be caused by one other event. Synchronicity entails an

underlying pattern of meaning that transcends physical causality. For more details, see: Roderick Main, "Religion, Science, and Synchronicity," Harvest: Journal for Jungian Studies, Vol. 46(2), 2000, pp. 89-107.

Chapter 13

[1] You may even know that the force of gravity is directly proportional to the masses of the objects involved – like the earth and whatever is falling to the earth – and inversely proportional to the square of the distance between the objects. But that is just a useful, operational description of gravity's effects, not of *how* it does what it does. The furthest we have gone in explaining gravity is the idea that it works by bending the fabric of space-time. Naturally, the next obvious question is *what* the fabric of space-time is, to begin with.

[2] Carl G. Jung, "The Undiscovered Self," Routledge, 2002.

[3] Jacques Vallée, "Passport to Magonia: From Folklore to Flying Saucers," Neville Spearman, 1970, p. 163.

BOOKS

ACADEMIC AND SPECIALIST

Iff Books publishes non-fiction. It aims to work with
authors and titles that augment our understanding of the
human condition, society and civilisation, and the world
or universe in which we live.
If you have enjoyed this book, why not tell other readers
by posting a review on your preferred book site.

Is There an Afterlife?
David Fontana

Is there an Afterlife? If so what is it like? How do Western ideas of the afterlife compare with Eastern? David Fontana presents the historical and contemporary evidence for survival of physical death.

Paperback: 978-1-90381-690-5

Nothing Matters
A Book About Nothing
Ronald Green

Thinking about Nothing opens the world to everything by illuminating new angles to old problems and stimulating new ways of thinking.

Paperback: 978-1-84694-707-0 ebook: 978-1-78099-016-3

Panpsychism
The Philosophy of the Sensuous Cosmos
Peter Ells

Are free will and mind chimeras? This book, anti-materialistic but respecting science, answers: No! Mind is foundational to all existence.

Paperback: 978-1-84694-505-2 ebook: 978-1-78099-018-7

Punk Science
Inside the Mind of God
Manjir Samanta-Laughton

Many have experienced unexplainable phenomena; God, psychic abilities, extraordinary healing and angelic encounters. Can cutting-edge science actually explain phenomena previously thought of as 'paranormal'?

Paperback: 978-1-90504-793-2

The Vagabond Spirit of Poetry
Edward Clarke
Spend time with the wisest poets of the modern age and of the
past, and let Edward Clarke remind you of the importance of
poetry in our industrialized world.
Paperback: 978-1-78279-370-0 ebook: 978-1-78279-369-4

Readers of ebooks can buy or view any of these bestsellers
by clicking on the live link in the title. Most titles are
published in paperback and as an ebook. Paperbacks are
available in traditional bookshops. Both print and
ebook formats are available online.

Find more titles and sign up to our readers' newsletter at
http://www.johnhuntpublishing.com/non-fiction

Follow us on Facebook at
https://www.facebook.com/JHPNonFiction
and Twitter at https://twitter.com/JHPNonFiction